Contents

KT-446-148

5689
X 10
156890

Hi
Pluke

Introduction

So, you'd like to do magic tricks? Why?

If your answer is you'd like to perform in front of audiences at home or school, or even at parties or community festivals, read on, and we'll give you some great tips to create a captivating magic show.

If you just like the idea of learning some magic tricks to do in front of your family and close friends, that's fine, too. Either way, this is the book for you, because there are so many tricks—101 in fact—contained in these pages, you will be able to keep everyone entertained for months!

Magic features in the myths and legends of cultures throughout the world. You may have heard of Merlin the Magician, who, it was said, trained King Arthur to become King of England more than 1,500 years ago. It was only Arthur who could pull the magic sword, Excalibur, from the rock in which Merlin had sunk it, and so he became king.

Although most of us can't explain how a microchip powers a computer or remember the principles of electricity once our science lesson is over, we readily accept what these and other marvels of technology can do for us. But who hasn't looked on in awe as a smiling magician makes a coin disappear or appear, seemingly at will? We love mysteries, and that's the appeal of magic.

Therefore, the first rule a magician must learn is: Never, ever tell anyone how to do a trick. It doesn't matter if the person is your best friend.

DO NOT TELL HOW A TRICK IS DONE!

Getting Started

There are a few rules to remember when performing magic tricks:

1 Never tell anyone how a trick is done. I know we've said this before, but it's the most important rule. DO NOT TELL!

2 Practice each trick in your repertoire until you know it perfectly and can do it over and over without a mistake.

3 Keep your audience directly in front of you. Don't let people sit beside or behind you.

4 Don't repeat a trick in front of the same audience. It may be flattering to be asked to do so, but the members of your audience are really only trying to see how the trick's done!

5 As a general rule, don't tell your audience what you are going to do. It's better to let anticipation and suspense build as you perform your trick. You can, however, talk to your audience. Talking, or patter, will help distract them, so they will not see what you are really doing!

6 Use expressions and gestures to enhance your act. For example, you can frown to show you are concentrating hard; or stand still without speaking to gain your audience's attention; or you might like to use sweeping arm gestures when you are calling upon your "magical powers" or trying to distract your audience.

7 Make sure all your props are in perfect working order and look good—no scruffy wands or hats.

8 Once you have learned a trick and can perform it, you may choose to alter it. This can be fun!

9 Practice and perfect the story or patter you tell while performing each trick—it's what makes you different from another person who performs the same trick.

10 Perform against a dark background under a good light.

Putting on a Magic Show

Begin by learning simple tricks that interest you and require only a few props. You will find these tricks are the easiest to perform. As you become more confident, you can learn longer, more difficult tricks.

Then it will be time to plan your act!

Every well-planned act has a beginning, a middle, and an end. When planning your act, remember to place shorter tricks between longer ones, as this will help to hold your audience's interest. Think about how long you want your show to be. When you are starting out, a good show is often a short show! Maybe you only want your show to last 10-15 minutes—that's still a lot of talking and a lot of tricks when you are new to magic!

Preparation

Apart from the obvious—learning your tricks so you are really confident performing them—you need to have the props for every trick you will perform. It is a good idea to cover a table with a cloth and put the props on top of the cloth until they are needed. Make sure your props look good!

Plan what you are going to wear. Dressing up as a magician, even if you don't rely on your costume for props, is a way of really making you feel the part. You may need to wear something special for certain tricks, such as a jacket for the arm-stretching trick.

Also, if you have decided to weave a special story or line of patter throughout the show, practice this as much as your tricks. You need to be confident with everything!

Performing

When you are in front of your audience, act confident. Look excited about the magic tricks you are performing. Take your bows and enjoy the applause—that's one of the reasons you are there.

Speak as clearly as you can—if you mumble, your audience won't be able to follow what you are saying and may miss crucial pieces of information.

Always involve your audience by asking for volunteers and don't worry if something goes wrong. Either repeat it, if appropriate, or begin the next trick.

Plan your show so your best trick is performed last and you go out on a cheer!

Finally, have fun!

Now... I need a family member to happily step forward to volunteer for this next trick!

Quick Tricks and Simple Illusions

Begin your show with a couple of these quick and simple illusions. They will leave your audience wanting more!

Trick 1
Long or Short

★ **You need:** a pencil, a piece of paper, a ruler

This is an easy illusion to warm up your audience.

1 Draw two straight, parallel lines on the paper, making sure they are exactly the same length, say 2 in. (5 cm) each. Position them about 1 in. (2 cm) apart.

2 Then draw angles (as in the diagrams to the right) on the ends of each line. You know the lines are the same length, but it will be hard to convince your friends because an optical illusion makes one appear shorter than the other.

Step back my friends! This is a Magic Rabbit... ...it could be loaded!

Did you know?
Mandrake the Magician was a popular comic strip hero of the 1940s. He would often outwit his opponents by using his magical powers.

MAGIC TRICKS

Trick 2
Magical Number Nine

★ **You need:** just a pair of hands—yours!

It's a good idea to create a story or patter about the magical number nine for this one!

1 Did you know you can multiply by 9 easily, just using your fingers? Hold your hands up and, in your head, number your fingers from 1 to 10, starting with your left thumb.

2 Whichever number you wish to multiply by 9, bend down the finger with that number. How many fingers are left standing on either side? For example, to multiply 5 by 9, bend finger number 5 and count the fingers to the left and right of it. The answer is 4 on your left hand and 5 on your right hand; this is 45—correct!

3 Try it with any multiple—up to 10, of course—it works every time!

Trick 3
More Nines

★ **You need:** a pencil, a piece of paper, a calculator (optional)

Keep up the illusion of nine being a magical number with this number trick.

9
18
27
36
45
54
63
72
81
+ 90
495

1 First, write down the number 9. Then underneath, in a column, write down the multiples of 9. That is, 9 multiplied by 2, then by 3, and so on, up to 9 multiplied by 10. (You will know an easy way of doing this if you did the trick before this one!) Draw a line underneath these figures.

2 Add all the numbers together and you should get 495. Add these digits together, 4 + 9 + 5, and the answer is 18—and by adding these digits together, 1 + 8, what do you get? Yes, 9!

3 Even if you add more multiples of 9 to the column, you will always end up with the same answer: 9. It's a spooky number, isn't it?

MAGIC TRICKS

Trick 4
Mind Reading

★ **You need:** a pencil, a piece of paper, a calculator (optional)

Again, this mind-reading trick uses the "magical" number nine. Performed with the help of a friend, this trick will greatly enhance your act and impress your audience!

1 Tell your friend to write down any three-digit number he or she likes, but the digits must decrease in value, such as 9, 7, and 2. Your friend must not let you see what's written.

2 Then tell your friend to write the same number backward underneath the first—that would be 2, 7, and 9.

3 Now your friend must subtract this number from the first and tell you only the final digit. In our example, this is 3.

4 You will immediately be able to say that the remaining numbers are 6 and 9. The middle digit is always 9, no matter what three-digit number your friend chose. (There's that sneaky 9 again!) You subtract the 3 from the 9 to find the first digit—that will be 6.

Trick 5
More Mind Reading

★ **You need:** a pencil, a piece of paper, a calculator

Tricks that involve mind reading and numbers are always fascinating. Here's another easy and effective one to include in your show.

1 Ask a friend to write down a number. It can be any number (it doesn't matter how many digits), provided the digits do not decrease in value. Your friend should not show you the number until the end of the trick.

```
15689
X 10
156890
```

2 Ask your friend to multiply the number she wrote down by 10. (Let's pretend your friend chose the number 15689.)

3 Ask your friend to subtract the first number from the second number.

```
156890
-15689
141201
```

MAGIC TRICKS

$$141201$$
$$+ 9$$
$$141210$$

4 Ask your friend to add 9 to the answer.

5 Ask your friend to cross out any number except a zero and tell you what the remaining digits are. In our example, the second 1 is crossed out and the remaining numbers are 1, 4, 2, 1, and 0.

$$14\cancel{1}210$$

6 You add these remaining digits in your head—they come to 8—and then subtract the total from 9 to find out what number was crossed out.

7 Tell your friend the number she crossed out was 1! Mind reading wins again!

Trick 6
Arrow-cadabra

★ **You need:** a pencil, a sheet of paper, a glass (straight-sided), a jug of water, a table

This *magic* trick is a great one to do before a small audience.

1 Fold the sheet of paper in half and draw an arrow in the middle of one side.

2 Stand the folded sheet on a table with the arrow facing the audience. Place the empty glass in front of it. Now challenge a member of the audience to turn the arrow around without touching the paper or the glass.

MAGIC TRICKS

3 Of course, he can't do it unless, unhappily, he has seen the trick done before! You do it by producing the jug of water (which until now has been out of sight) and filling the glass with water.

4 Presto! The arrow turns to face the opposite way!

Now... don't take your eyes off this cabbage for a second ... as it's about to disappear!

My... what's that over there?

Did you know?

Magicians are often very theatrical performers, more so than actors! Magicians use grand gestures to distract audiences from what is really happening during a show!

Trick 7
Magic Paper Rings

★ **You need:** a paper strip about 12 in. (30 cm) by 1.5 in. (4 cm), glue, scissors

This quick little illusion will have your audience believing you can do anything!

1 Hold the paper strip and twist it once.

2 Then glue the ends together.

3 Cut around the center of the ring carefully. What's the result? Two rings? No, it's one big ring if you've cut correctly.

4 Now to take this a little further—cut around the center again. Do you think you'll get a really big ring this time? No! This time there are two rings!

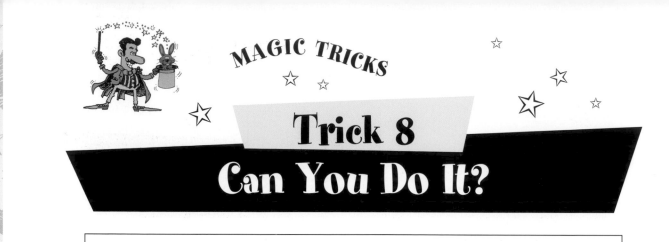

MAGIC TRICKS

Trick 8
Can You Do It?

★ **You need:** a sheet of paper, an unopened can of food, a table

You can only show this trick once to any group, as you give the game away each time.

1 Lay the sheet of paper flat on the table and put the can on top of it (right in the middle).

2 Challenge anyone in the audience to remove the paper without touching the can or allowing it to tip over. No one will be able to do it—unless, of course, someone has seen the trick performed elsewhere! But you can!

3 Pick up the longer side of the paper and begin to roll it into a tube. As the paper tube reaches the can, keep rolling. Do not touch the can. The tube will move the can away from you. Keep on rolling the paper until the can has moved completely off the paper and you can wave your rolled tube in a salute!

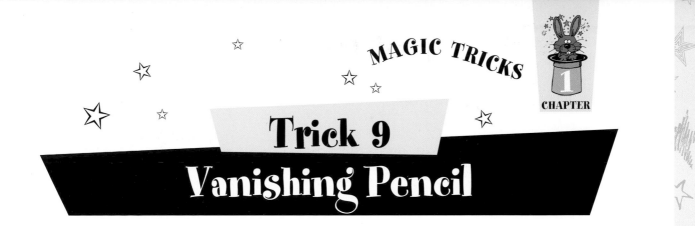

Trick 9
Vanishing Pencil

★ **You need:** a coin, a blunt pencil

Tell your audience you can make a coin disappear—but it seems you need more practice!

1 Stand with your left side toward your audience if you are right-handed or your right side toward them if you are left-handed. Put the coin in the hand closest to the audience and hold it up, explaining that it will disappear once you tap it sharply three times with your pencil.

2 Hold the end of the pencil with the fingers of your other hand and bring it up into the air until it is level with your ear.

ONE!

3 Bring the pencil down and tap the coin sharply with it while exclaiming a really loud "One!"

MAGIC TRICKS

4 Do this again—bringing the pencil up to exactly the same height and down again, tapping the coin and saying "Two!"

THREE!

5 Without missing a beat, bring the pencil up one more time, this time sliding it easily and quickly behind your ear. Bring your now-empty hand down, saying "Three!", and look really surprised to discover the pencil has vanished.

6 Turn away from the audience, without showing the pencil if possible, and mutter something about having to go and practice the trick more.

7 Remember—to succeed with this trick you need to keep the same "beat" going when counting. Don't pause between any of the taps of the coin, especially not before the third tap!

Hey... I'm not a happy Pharoah...! What happened to the Vanishing Pyramid Trick and turning a camel into a palm tree?

Did you know?

The first record of performing magicians is in the Westcar Papyrus in the State Museum of Berlin, Germany. It contains documented proof that magicians performed for the Pharaohs of ancient Egypt about 4500 years ago.

Trick 10
The Coin Really Disappears This Time...

> ★ **You need:** a coin, a pencil, a table

This trick follows on beautifully from the previous one, but can be a stand-alone trick if you prefer.

1 Begin by sitting at a table with your side to the audience. If your dominant hand (that is the hand you do most things with) is your right hand, sit with your left hand toward the audience, and vice versa if you are left-handed.

2 Repeat trick 9 (but stay seated). When you count "Three!", act surprised the pencil has vanished and look questioningly at the audience. At first they'll be surprised, but then you should let them see the pencil stuck behind your ear, and they'll begin laughing. You should laugh, too.

THREE!

Quick Tricks and Simple Illusions

23

MAGIC TRICKS

3 Reach up with your dominant hand to remove the pencil. Now here's the clever bit: while you are removing the pencil with one hand (and hopefully the whole audience is watching you do that), the hand holding the coin quickly tips it into your lap.

4 As the coin leaves your hand, close your hand into a fist (you want the audience to think you are still holding the coin).

5 Say something along the lines of: "Well, I tricked you there, but now let me really make the coin disappear." Lift the pencil and tap your closed fist with it, then open your hand to show the coin has gone!

Trick 11
It's Always 1089

> ★ **You need:** two pieces of paper, an envelope,
> a pencil, a table, a calculator (optional)

With this quick trick, you'll convince your audience you have special powers!

1 Place your props on the table and stand in front of your audience. Talk about the power of the mind—about telepathy and thought reading. Say something like: "There is always someone in *my* audience whose *mind* is open to me." Then stop and say there is someone in the audience whose thoughts you are picking up right now. Point to a person in the audience.

2 Pretend to be thinking hard, and ask the "telepathic" person to concentrate on transmitting his thoughts to you. Say you think a number is coming through to you. Quickly write down 1089 on a piece of paper, place it in the envelope, and seal it.

MAGIC TRICKS

3 Hand the other piece of paper and the pencil to the "telepathic" person and ask him to write down any three-digit number in which all the digits are different. (In our example, we've used the number 341.) Now ask him to reverse the number and subtract the smaller from the larger one. Ask him to write down a three-digit answer even if the first digit is zero.

4 He now needs to reverse this last number and add the last two numbers together. Ask him to read his answer out loud to the rest of the audience. Now ask him to open the envelope and read the number you wrote down. Both numbers will be 1089.

Boy.... That's really spooky! How does she do it?

5 The number is always 1089, so you only want to do this trick once in front of the same audience!

Trick 12
Pocket Puzzler

★ **You need:** a deck of cards, a calculator,
a piece of paper, a pencil

Using your magical powers, you are able to name the card hidden in an assistant's pocket.

1 Ask a volunteer to come forward and write down any four-digit number on a piece of paper, without letting you see any of the numbers. The only condition is the four numbers must be different. (In our example, we'll use the number 7539.)

2 Ask him to add the four numbers together and write down the total. Now give him the calculator and ask him to subtract the total from the original number.

7 + 5 + 3 + 9 = 24

$$\begin{array}{r} 7539 \\ -24 \\ \hline 7515 \end{array}$$

3 Hand the volunteer a deck of cards and ask him to secretly remove four cards that have the same numbers as the four digits in his answer. (An ace = 1 and a king = 0.) Each card must be a different suit.

MAGIC TRICKS

4 Ask your volunteer to put one card (that isn't a king) in his pocket, or out of sight, and hand you the other three cards. In our example, the volunteer puts the five of clubs in his pocket.

5 Now you must mentally add the values of the three cards. If the answer has more than one digit, add those digits until there is only one digit. (For example, 13 becomes 1 + 3 = 4).

$$7 + 1 + 5 = 13$$
$$1 + 3 = 4$$
$$9 - 4 = 5$$

6 Mentally subtract this number from 9, and the value of the card in your volunteer's pocket will appear, as if by magic! It's a 5—and because you are holding cards that are hearts, spades, and diamonds—the card must be the 5 of clubs!

7 The only exception to this clever little trick is when you mentally subtract the value of the cards from 9 and the answer is 0—the missing card isn't a king, it's a 9.

that's amazing!

Diabolically Clever Card Tricks

Many young magicians include card tricks in their magic shows. This is a good idea. Nearly every household has a deck or two of cards lying about, so no extra money needs to be spent on props, and there are many simple card tricks you can learn that look great when performed!

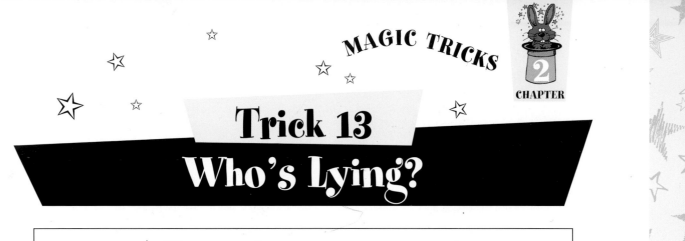

Trick 13
Who's Lying?

★ **You need:** a deck of cards, a table

Card tricks are a magician's stock-in-trade. Everyone expects you to be able to flip, shuffle, twist, and "read" cards telepathically—so let's get on with it!

1 Before your audience arrives, shuffle the deck of cards. Make sure you know which card is on the bottom.

2 Once your audience is seated, fan out the deck of cards on the table in front of you and ask a volunteer to choose one card. She is not to show or tell you its identity.

3 While the volunteer looks at the card, you should close the fan of cards, straighten the deck, and place it on the table, facedown. Ask the volunteer to cut the deck into two equal piles and put her card on the pile she cut from the top of the deck.

MAGIC TRICKS

4 Now ask your volunteer to place the other half of the deck on top of this. This should mean the card you memorized, which was at the bottom of the pile a minute ago, is now on top of the selected card.

5 Now is the time for some good magician's patter. Explain to the audience the deck of cards is special—it can detect lies!

6 Explain to your volunteer that you are going to turn each card over and ask her if this is the card she selected. She is to say "No" every time, even when you turn over her selected card. The deck of cards will "tell" you when she is lying. Obviously, you are looking for the card you memorized—the card after it will be the selected card.

My magic pack of cards tells me you might be telling fibbies!

7 When you turn over the selected card and your volunteer says "No," yell "Liar!" loudly and watch her reaction!

Trick 14
Find the Queen

> ★ **You need: five playing cards (four black cards and one red queen), glue, a clothespin**

This trick is really an optical illusion. All your volunteer has to do is find the queen—but it's harder to do than it seems.

1 Before facing your audience, you need to prepare the cards. Arrange them in an overlapping line—first, three black cards, then the red queen, then the fourth black card. Now glue them in place and leave them overnight to dry.

2 Once your audience arrives, show them the strip of cards, pointing out the red queen. Ask a volunteer to remember where it is.

3 After handing the volunteer the clothespin, turn the cards around so the backs of the cards face the audience. Ask your volunteer to clip the clothespin onto the queen.

4 Once he has clipped the pin onto a card, turn the strip of cards around. Your volunteer will be astonished to see his guess wasn't right because this looks so easy to do! More than likely (and you can test this yourself), the card that was pinned was the last card.

Trick 15
Balancing Act

★ **You need:** one playing card, a plastic cup (not glass!)

Simple tricks are good tricks! Practice this one and you'll look like the greatest magician—and don't forget your patter. This is the story you tell while performing magic—it's exclusively yours, even if the tricks are old!

1 Hold the card with the face (that is, the suit and number) toward the audience. If you are right-handed, hold it in your left hand; if you are left-handed, hold it in your right hand. Your thumb should be on one side of the card, and the middle, ring, and little fingers on the other. Your forefinger or index finger rests behind the card.

2 With your other hand, and while talking constantly to your audience about your magical powers, gently place the cup on top of the card. Place it so that three-quarters of the cup is behind the card, and hold the cup steady with your index finger.

3 From the front it looks as though the cup is just sitting there, perfectly balanced—as indeed it is, on your finger!

34

Trick 16
The Mysterious Missing Card

★ **You need:** a deck of cards (with a piece of double-sided adhesive tape on the back of the top card), a table

It doesn't matter which card your volunteer chooses from the pack—you can make it disappear immediately with this trick.

DOUBLE-SIDED TAPE

1 Stand facing your audience with the deck of cards in your hand. Fan out the cards between both hands, so the faces of the cards are facing your audience. (This also hides the piece of tape on the back of the top card.)

2 Select one person from the audience to study the cards. Ask her to take a card from the deck.

3 Once she has chosen a card, close the fan of cards and hold the deck upright, still showing the face of the cards to the audience. If you are left-handed, hold the deck in your right hand. If you are right-handed, hold the deck in your left hand.

MAGIC TRICKS

4 While you were doing this, your volunteer should have shown everyone else the card she chose. Now you take it back with your free hand, keeping the face away from you, and place it with a flourish back on to the deck—right on top of the double-sided adhesive tape! Make sure it's squarely on top so it looks as if there is only one card there.

5 Now, place the deck facedown on the table and cut the cards. Explain to your audience that you are going to make the chosen card disappear. Say, "Sim Sala Bim!" or wave your hands or snap your fingers before turning over the cards and spreading them out on the table. Ask your volunteer to find the card she chose earlier. Of course, she cannot. The card has disappeared! Take a bow!

SIM SALA BIM all right! It must be some kind of trick!

6 If you prefer, you can keep the cards in your hands, cut them, and then count them out onto the top of the table—of course, there will be only 51, and the chosen card will have "vanished."

Trick 17
The Chosen Card

★ **You need:** a deck of cards, a table

This trick requires some preparation, but when it's done properly, it's a real winner!

1 Separate the cards by color. Make a pile of red cards and a pile of black cards. Put one pile on top of the other, so you now have a deck of cards separated into two colored halves. Now it's time to bring on the audience!

RED PILE   BLACK PILE

2 Pick up the cards and hold the deck facedown in your left palm if you are right-handed and in your right palm if you are left-handed. With your other hand, begin to flick the cards with your thumb at the end nearest you. This way, you are the only one who can see the faces of the cards. Flick upward from the bottom of the deck.

You don't have to actually see the numbers and suits, you want to see when the colors change. While you are doing this, explain to the audience that you are going to cut the deck into two equal piles.

3 Once the color changes, you stop and cut the deck. Only you know that you have cut the deck into two equal piles of different-colored cards—your audience thinks you have just cut the cards into two roughly equal piles, especially when you say: "I think the piles look the same."

4 Ask for a volunteer.

5 Take one pile (let's say the red one), and spread the cards facedown in your hands and ask the volunteer to take a card and remember it. He can even show it to the rest of the audience if he wants to.

6 While he is doing that, put down those cards and pick up the other pile (in this case, the black one). Spread this one out in the same way and tell the volunteer to place the selected card into this half of the deck.

7 Put the cards together again to make one deck and ask the volunteer if he would like to cut the deck. He can do this as many times as he likes. (Because your volunteer placed a red card into the black half of the deck, it doesn't matter how many times the cards are cut. When you begin to look through the cards, you will see clusters of same-colored cards together. When you see one red card in a cluster of black cards, you will know this is the chosen card.) However, do not let your volunteer shuffle the cards—if he does, then you will not be able to find the chosen card!

8 It is possible that the chosen card will end up on the top or the bottom of the deck. If you cannot see a single red card in a black cluster, then check the top or bottom card. If you find a red card next to some black ones, it is the chosen card.

Trick 18
Keep Trying!

★ **You need:** a deck of cards, a table

This is one trick that relies on good patter. You need to keep your audience interested and intrigued even though you seem to be having trouble making the trick work. It also relies on good math skills! Read on...

1 To begin, deal seven over-lapping rows of three cards each. Deal them onto the table from left to right (this is important!) and faceup. Make sure you can see the number and suit of each card. Put the rest of the cards to one side—you won't need them for this trick.

2 Ask a volunteer to mentally choose a card, but not to name or touch the card, as you will guess it. Then pretend to study the cards, as though trying to magically sense which one has been selected.

3 Tell your volunteer you seem to be having trouble magically sensing the card. Ask her to tell you which column it is in.

4 When she tells *you* which column, pick up each of the three columns. You must pick the columns up so that the column with the selected card is stacked between the other two.

STEP A.

STEP B.

5 Deal the cards again, exactly as before. Frown and pretend to be searching for the right card. You still can't find it! Ask your volunteer again which column the card is in, then repeat step 4.

6 Repeat step 5.

7 By now, you should be acting as though you are very annoyed! So say to your audience you will try it one last time.

8 Begin dealing the cards as before, but this time, as you are dealing, silently count to yourself until you reach the number 11. Then stop suddenly, smile with relief, and hold up the card, announcing, "This is it!"

1, 2, 3, 4,
5, 6, 7, 8,
9, 10, ...
11

9 This trick depends on mathematics, so you need to follow the directions exactly. It will work every time, but it's a good idea to try it on your own to test it out!

Trick 19
The Talking Cards

★ **You need:** a deck of cards with no jokers, a table

You can find any card in a deck by listening to your "talking" cards...

1 Explain to your audience that you have special powers that enable you to hear "talking" cards—even though they won't be able to hear anything!

2 Ask a volunteer to deal out the cards faceup on the table. He must deal them out in a single row until you say: "Stop." You should mentally count the number of cards being dealt, taking note of the seventh card. When your volunteer reaches 26, tell him to stop and say something like: "That should be enough cards to choose from."

3 Now tell the audience you'll select a card at random from those on the table. Pretend to consider the cards, then point to the seventh card. Ask your volunteer to tell the audience the name of the selected card. Explain to your audience that you will be able to find the selected card again with the help of your "talking" cards.

4 Pick up the cards in the same order they were dealt, stacking the second card on top of the first and so on. Put the stack of cards facedown on the table and put the rest of the deck facedown on top.

5 Slowly deal out the cards, so that they lie faceup in a column. Tell the audience the cards are "talking" to you. Note the number of the first card. Continue to deal and silently count from that number until you reach 10. For example, if the first card is a 4, the next card becomes 5, then 6, 7, 8, 9, and 10—no matter what the numbers on the cards actually are.

6 Once you reach number 10, start another column—all the while pretending the cards are "talking" to you. If the first card you turn over in a column is a 10 or a face card, such as a king or queen, it counts as 10, and you must begin the next column. Aces count as 1.

7 Make three columns and then stop. Stare at the cards and while the audience thinks you are "listening" to them, mentally add up the three cards at the tops of the columns. Perhaps these are 10, 3, and 2, which would make 15. This number is the key to finding the selected card!

what's that you say?

8 Now tell the audience the cards have told you the location of the selected card. Tell the volunteer to deal off the same number of cards as your total—in our example, that is 15. The fifteenth card will be your selected card! The volunteer and audience will be amazed!

9 Try this trick a few times on your own or for your parents and see how easy it is!

Trick 20
Choices

★ **You need:** a deck of cards, a table

In this trick, you ask a volunteer to deal you a card seemingly at random—but, in fact, you already know the card's identity!

1 Before your show, memorize the tenth card from the top of a deck of cards.

2 Begin the trick by giving a volunteer the deck of cards. Ask her to think of a number between 10 and 20, then ask her to deal that number of cards facedown into a stack on the table. The rest of the deck can be put aside.

3 Now your volunteer needs to add together the two digits that make up the number she selected. If she selected the number 14, for example, she would add 1 and 4 to get 5. She then deals that number of cards, 5, from the stack and looks at the fifth card without telling anyone what it is. This card will be the card you memorized before the trick—the original tenth card.

4 Pretend to read the volunteer's mind. Perhaps you'd like to heighten the drama by drawing the card on a piece of paper. Or you could ask the volunteer to return the card to the deck and shuffle the cards. She hands the deck to you and you "select" the card by "reading her fingerprints!"

5 However you do it, you'll be right every time!

MAGIC TRICKS

Trick 21
ESP Card

★ **You need:** a deck of cards, an envelope, a card from another deck of cards

In this trick, you hold a sealed envelope up before your audience and tell them there is a card inside. You then select a card—seemingly at random—and it matches the card inside the sealed envelope!

 1 Before your audience arrives, find the card (we'll call it card 1) in the full deck that matches the single card (card 2) you have taken from another deck. Place card 1 tenth from the top in the deck.

 2 Seal card 2 in the envelope.

 3 Introduce this trick by telling your audience there is a card in the sealed envelope. Ask a volunteer to hold the sealed envelope.

 4 Hand the full deck to another volunteer and ask him to select a card as in Trick 20. The final card dealt will be card 1, which, of course, matches the card in the envelope.

 5 Ask the first volunteer to open the envelope, and everyone will be sure you have special powers.

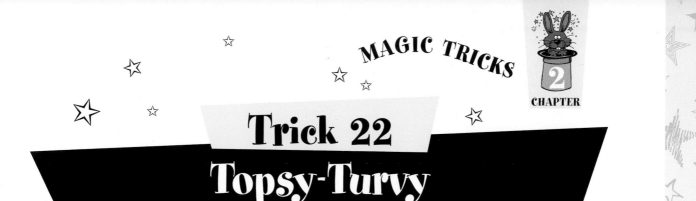

Trick 22
Topsy-Turvy

★ **You need:** a deck of cards, a table, a wand (optional)

Make a magician out of a volunteer with this trick. Your volunteer will pick a card, place it back in the deck, wave a magic wand—and presto!—the card will have magically turned over in the deck!

1 Before the audience arrives, turn over the bottom card in the deck so the deck looks the same from both ends.

2 From your audience, select a volunteer. Then fan out the cards facedown in your hands, taking care not to show the reversed card on the bottom of the deck. Ask your volunteer to select a card and show it to the audience, but not to you.

3 As the volunteer is showing the card to the audience, you should close the deck in the palm of one hand and secretly turn it over so that the reversed bottom card is now on top of the deck. You need to practice this movement to make it so smooth that no one will notice you doing it.

4 Ask your volunteer to place the card facedown anywhere she likes in the deck that you are still holding. What she's done, of course, is place the selected card backward in the deck of cards.

MAGIC TRICKS

5 Now tell the volunteer she is going to perform the magic trick with the help of your magic wand (if you have one) or some magic words that you will tell her. Turn over the hand holding the deck, so it is now palm down, and put the deck of cards flat on the table. Now the deck is right-side up again with the reversed card on the bottom of the deck. The selected card is also reversed.

6 Once your volunteer has woven her magic spell over the cards, you can fan out the cards on the table or move them from hand to hand until you come to the selected card, which, of course, will be reversed faceup within the deck. Show the audience the card. Congratulate your new assistant and take the applause with her!

Did you know?

In England, in the early 1700s, magic was considered respectable entertainment. Magicians performed in private homes, at booths at village fairs, and in theatres.

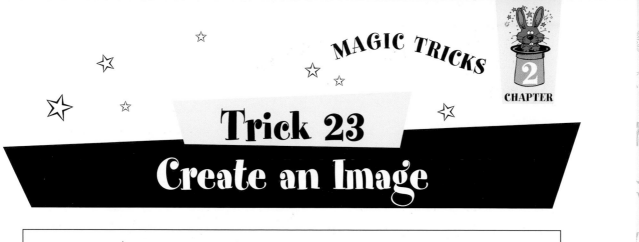

Trick 23
Create an Image

★ **You need:** a deck of cards in its box, a small mirror, glue, a table

This trick relies on a good setup!

1 Before your audience arrives, glue a small makeup mirror on the back of the box of cards. This may need to dry overnight. Keep the deck of cards in the box, with the flap closed.

2 To begin your performance, hold the box of cards in one hand with the mirror facing toward you. Remove the deck of cards with the other hand and fan out the cards facedown on the table. Keep hold of the box.

3 Ask someone in the audience to choose a card, look at it, memorize it, and then hand it to you. The card face must be turned away from you. (You are still holding the box and may need to mention this in the patter you devise for the trick.)

MAGIC TRICKS

4 Take the card, making sure the face is still turned toward the audience and your volunteer, and say something like: "I need the help of the magic box to sense the suit and number of the card." Then move the card behind the box so it is possible for you to glimpse the card in the mirror.

5 Keep the patter going by asking your volunteer to concentrate on the card he chose and to send a mental image of it to you. Place the box on the table (once you know what the card is!), ensuring the mirror can't be seen, and put the card on top of the box so it will release its magic powers. Then proudly tell the audience what card the volunteer chose!

That's it... CONCENTRATE really hard on that card... I SEE IT NOW... I SEE THE CARD!

6 Don't do this trick more than once before the same audience, as it is too easy for someone to ask why you are holding on to the box. Someone may even see the mirror!

Trick 24
Arise Card

★ **You need:** a deck of cards

Make any card you name rise out of the deck.

1 Ask a volunteer to shuffle the deck of cards.

2 When the deck is handed back to you, straighten it, taking note of which card is facedown on top. Perhaps it is the ten of diamonds.

3 Hold the deck vertically in one hand (left if you are right-handed and right if you are left-handed), so the cards are facing the audience.

PUSH ON AND UPWARDS WITH THIS FINGER

4 Place your other hand behind the deck and rest your forefinger or index finger on top of the deck. Now extend your little finger (or ring finger if it is easier) until it touches the back of the top card (the ten of diamonds).

5 Now all you need to do is name the card and ask it to rise for you! "Ten of diamonds... arise now from your slumber!" While you are saying this, push upward on the top card with your little or ring finger. Do it slowly, making sure your forefinger or index finger is rising as you speak. From where the audience is sitting, it will look as if your forefinger or index finger is encouraging the rising card to rise, and it will also look as if the card is coming from the middle of the deck. Easy, but effective!

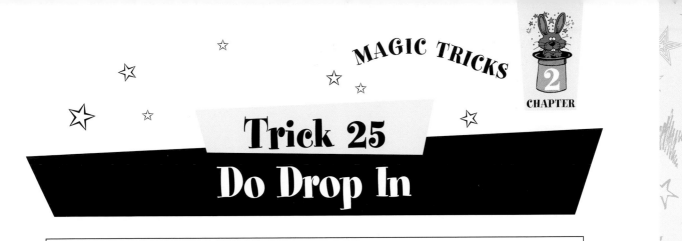
Trick 25
Do Drop In

★ **You need:** a deck of cards, a hat

This is another simple trick that is easy to set up and perform. It's a good one to do at the beginning of a magic show.

1 Ask for a volunteer to act as your assistant. Give your assistant half the deck of cards.

2 Place the hat upside down on the floor in front of you. Take a card and hold it 4 ft. (1.2 m) above the center of the hat. Tell your audience you bet you can get more cards into the hat than your assistant can.

4 ft. (1.2 m)

3 Take a card and hold it by one of the short edges. You are just demonstrating how to drop the cards into the hat; if you actually let yours go, it probably won't go in the hat, and everyone will laugh! That's OK—in fact, that's really good!

4 Now get your assistant to drop her cards into the hat one at a time. The majority of the cards will miss the hat and fall onto the floor. When your assistant has no more cards left, count the cards that have made it into the hat. Pick up the cards that didn't get into the hat and make a big noise about how poorly your assistant did!

5 Now you get to show off—and win the bet! Hold your cards flat between your fingers and thumb, facing the floor. As you drop each card, it will fall straight down (not float and spin as before). If you are standing directly over the hat, plan on nine out of ten cards going in the hat!

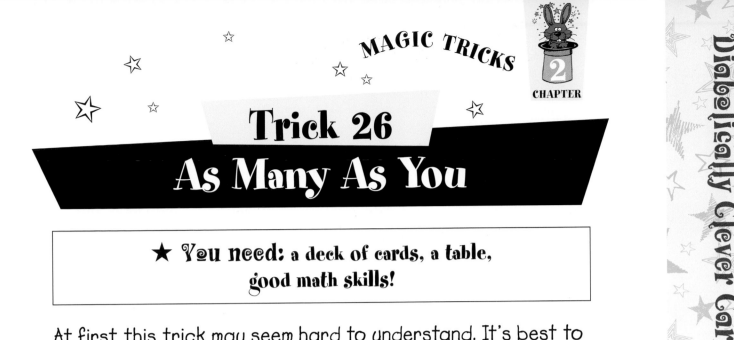

Trick 26
As Many As You

★ **You need:** a deck of cards, a table, good math skills!

At first, this trick may seem hard to understand. It's best to practice the trick while reading the instructions.

1 Place the cards on the table and ask a volunteer to remove a small bunch of them. Watch and try to estimate how many cards he takes.

2 You now take a bunch of cards yourself. Make sure it's more than your volunteer took.

3 Ask your volunteer to count his cards while you turn your back. He must count silently. While your back is turned, you also count your cards silently and accurately.

4 Perhaps you have 16 cards. Now you need to use your math skills. Subtract any number from 1 to 5 from your total; let's say you subtract 4, and your new total is 12.

MAGIC TRICKS

5 What you now say to your volunteer is: "I bet I have as many cards as you, plus 4 extra (the number between 1 and 5 you chose), and enough left over to make yours equal 12 (your new total)."

6 The volunteer tells you how many cards he has, and you deal from your pile this exact number. So if your volunteer has 10 cards, you deal out 10 cards. You now say: "That's the number of cards you had." Deal 4 more cards, counting out loud, and say "That's the four extra", and finally deal out what's left in your hand. In our example, it should be 2 cards. These 2 cards plus the number of cards your volunteer had in the beginning add up to 12.

7 It sounds complicated, but the more you practice the trick on your own, the easier it will become—and you'll find it works every time!

Trick 27
What's Gone?

★ **You need:** a deck of cards, a table, a chair

You'll need to concentrate while performing this trick. But do it well, and you'll earn yourself a reputation as a good magician.

 1 Hand one person in the audience nine cards in any suit—ace through 9.

 2 Ask your assistant to shuffle the cards. While he or she is shuffling, you should take a seat with your back to the table.

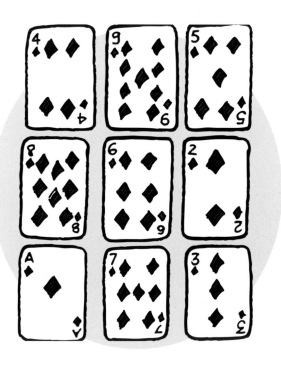

3 Tell your assistant to deal the cards into three rows with three cards in each.

4 Now ask your assistant to remove one card, show it to the audience, then put the card in his or her pocket.

5 The assistant now adds up the cards in the columns, ignoring the space where the removed card once was. In our example, the answers are 13, 15, and 10.

6 Your assistant now adds up the digits in the answers. In our example, that would be 1 + 3 + 1 + 5 + 1 + 0 = 11. Your assistant tells you the total, which in this case is 11. Without pausing or turning around to look at the cards or the audience, you press your fingers to your head and say: "You removed the 7."

7 You have deduced this answer on a simple mathematical basis. You always subtract the number given to you from the number 9, or a multiple of 9. For example, we know that 11 cannot be subtracted from 9, so for any number greater than 8 you subtract it from 18. Therefore, 18 - 11 = 7–presto! You're right! (Should the number be greater than 17, simply subtract it from 27.)

Trick 28
Card Telepathy

★ **You need:** a deck of cards

If you practice and perfect this illusion, it looks really impressive, but you do need to be able to memorize a couple of cards at a time. This is a great trick to begin a show... it makes you look so good!

1 First ask a person from your audience to shuffle the deck and then hand them back to you. Explain to your audience that you will use telepathy to "read" the card that is at the front of the deck facing them.

2 Now for the secret to your success. There are two things you do—first, you put the deck behind your back and, making sure the audience doesn't see you, you take the front card and move it to the back of the deck, facing in the reverse direction.

3 The next thing you do is have a "dummy" run, by saying to everyone: "Now this is what we're going to do!" Explain in more detail as you hold up the deck of cards with the reversed card facing the audience. Don't guess the card this time. Instead you memorize the card facing you.

4 Now, begin. Put the deck behind your back and move the card you memorized to the other side of the deck, facing in the reverse direction (as in step 2). Hold up the deck with the reversed card facing the audience and correctly name the card facing them. Each time you hold the deck up to the audience, facing you is the next card you will show them and the next card you will "guess" correctly. You must memorize it!

5 For this trick to work well, you need to string the audience along and not guess the card immediately. Pretend to be reading their minds as they concentrate on the card they can see. Say things like: "I feel it's a card with red vibrations" or "It's one of the lower-numbered cards in hearts." Press the fingers of your free hand to your forehead while "thinking."

All these vibrations... reading minds... and deep concentration is giving me a headache!

This is the last card!

6 Around three or four cards into the trick, say: "This will be the last card, because concentrating this hard always gives me a headache."

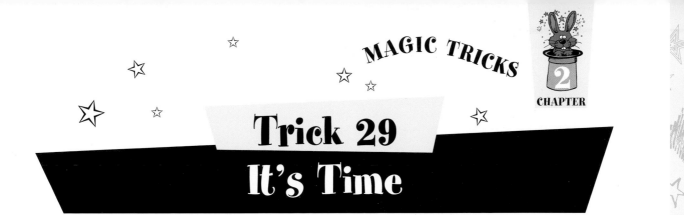

Trick 29
It's Time

★ **You need: a deck of cards, a watch**

When you begin this trick, you might like to make references to Alice in Wonderland and the White Rabbit, who was always looking at his watch and saying, "I'm late, I'm late, for a very important date." You will use your watch in this trick.

1 Ask four volunteers to choose a card each. All the volunteers should look at all the cards. You should not look at any of them.

2 The volunteers then discuss secretly which of the four cards they prefer, while you divide the rest of the cards into two equal facedown piles.

3 Ask the volunteers to hand you the chosen card. Do not look at it. Ask the volunteers which pile they want their chosen card to be placed upon. Place it there, then place the other three cards on the other pile.

MAGIC TRICKS

SINGLE CARD ON TOP

PILE WITH 3 CARDS ON TOP

4 Once this is done, you pick up the pile with the three cards on top and place it on top of the other pile, so the single chosen card is now in the middle of the deck.

5 The reference to the time is brought in now. You look at your watch and tell everyone it's 17 minutes past 11, for example. Ask a volunteer to add these numbers together—to get a total of 28—then deal out the cards to "magically" reveal the chosen card is in fact the 28th down in the deck!

Oh my.... Will you just look at the time ..! **17** minutes past **11** ! 17 + 11 = 28 Bet your card is **28**th down in the pack.

6 Of course, you can only use this trick when the time will add up to 28: at 12:16, 1:27, 2:26, 3:25, and so on.

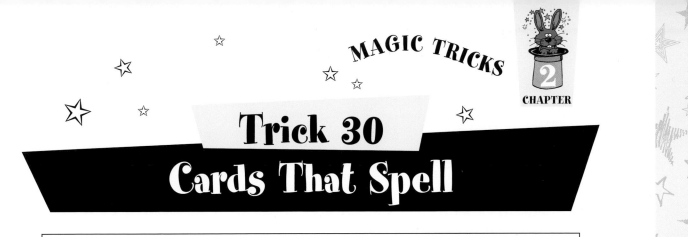

Trick 30
Cards That Spell

★ **You need:** a deck of cards, a table

Prove to your audience that cards can spell their own numbers! This trick–simple, but very effective–relies on the magician remembering the correct sequence when picking up the scattered cards.

1 You'll need to create some patter explaining that you've discovered cards can actually spell and you think spades (or whatever suit you choose) is the smartest suit .

2 Once you've selected your suit, take all 13 cards from the suit out of the deck. While doing this, place the 13 cards faceup on a table in a random, scattered way. If they are scattered fairly widely across the table, it will seem less likely you are actually going to pick them up in a particular order. Put the rest of the deck aside.

3 Now pick up the spades in the following order: queen, 4, ace, 8, king, 2, 7, 5, 10, jack, 3, 6, 9. (Make sure the queen is at the top of the pack when it is facedown, and the 9 is on the bottom.)

4 Now all you have to do is have fun and remember how to spell!

5 Begin by spelling out A-C-E. When you say "A," put the first card at the bottom of the pile. When you say "C," put the second card at the bottom of the pile. When you say "E," reveal the third card to be, in fact, the ace. This card is put aside.

6 Next spell out T-W-O in the same way. Again, when you get to the third card, you will turn up the 2. Put it aside on top of the ace.

7 Continue in this way, spelling out T-H-R-E-E, F-O-U-R, F-I-V-E, and so on, until the final card left is the king.

Trick 31
Find That Card

★ **You need:** a sharp pencil, a deck of cards

In this trick, you ask a volunteer to choose a card from the deck. After the volunteer has returned the card to the deck, you are able to "magically" locate it. This is a quick and effective trick that you can perform between two longer tricks for a change of pace.

1 The secret to this trick is that you carefully run a pencil line down one side of every card in the deck before the performance. This line needs to be dark enough for you to see and light enough so no one in the audience sees it!

PENCIL LINE

2 Fan out the cards facedown toward a member of the audience and ask him to select any card.

3 Ask your volunteer to show the card to the audience without looking at it. This is your opportunity to quickly and secretly turn the whole deck around. Have your volunteer slide the card back into the deck. Make sure the volunteer is putting

the card back in the same direction it was pointing when he took it. If you see that he's turned it, distract everyone with some patter and secretly turn the deck again.

4 Because the pack has now been reversed, the chosen card will be the only one showing a pencil mark against the plain white of one side of the pack. With your eagle eyes and your clever patter, it is an easy thing for you to break the pack at the selected card, remove it with a flourish, and show it to the audience. Then wait for the applause!

The only card with a line on the other side.

Trick 32
Always Red

★ **You need:** two decks of cards with different-colored designs on the back (one design should be red), a piece of paper, a pen or pencil, a table

As a magician, it's great to involve *your* audience. In this trick, you write a prediction on a piece of paper and give it to an audience member. The prediction states: "You will pick the only red card out of the six cards." And that's what happens!

1 You need to pick out six cards for this trick. One must be the ace of spades or clubs from the deck with the red design on the back. One must be the 6 of hearts or diamonds from the other deck, and the other four cards can be any clubs or spades from the same deck with values of 7 or greater.

2 Before your audience arrives, arrange the six chosen cards in the following order at the top of the deck (the one without the red design on the back): other, ace, 6, other, other, other.

3 Once your audience arrives, ask for a volunteer. As she stands with you at the table, write your prediction down and show her and the audience.

4 Next, deal the top six cards as follows: facedown, faceup, facedown, faceup, facedown, faceup.

RED BACK

SIX OF DIAMONDS

5 Now the volunteer gives you a number between 1 and 6—let's say she chooses 4. Remember you've predicted she will choose a red card, so count from right to left and you get to turn over the six of hearts or diamonds.

4   3   2   1

If the volunteer chooses 1, you pick up the ace and show the red-backed design. If she chooses 2, count from left to right and show the ace. For 3, count from left to right to get to the 6 of hearts or diamonds. For 5, count from right to left to get to the ace, and for 6, pick up the 6 of diamonds or hearts straightaway.

6 Don't do this trick again in the same show—it becomes too obvious you knew what cards were there!

Trick 33
Your Card Is...

★ **You need: a deck of cards**

This is another simple but effective trick to show you are a master or mistress of the cards! Yet again, you will find the "selected" card hidden in the deck. Remember to deal the cards the same way every time.

1 Deal out three piles with seven cards in each pile. Lay them out one, one, one, and two, two, two, rather than dealing one pile at a time. Put the remainder of the deck aside—it won't be needed.

2 Ask an audience member to pick a card from any pile and to remember it, but not tell anyone what it is. He should then put the card back in the same pile.

3 You now gather up the three piles of cards, making sure the pile with the selected card is between the other two piles, then deal them out again, into three groups of seven cards.

SELECTED PILE

①
②

4 Ask your volunteer to inspect each pile of cards and tell you which pile the selected card is now in.

5 Again gather all the piles of cards, keeping the selected card's pile between the other two piles, and deal them out into three groups of seven.

6 The volunteer again finds his selected card and indicates to you which pile it is now in. You gather the piles up, again keeping the selected card's pile between the other two.

Yes... don't worry... I even amaze myself!

7 Spell out Y-O-U-R-C-A-R-D-I-S by removing a card for each letter—and the next card will be the selected card!

Diabolically Clever Card Tricks

Trick 34
How Odd

★ **You need:** a deck of cards, a table

This is a great trick to perform in front of young children. Many older children and adults will realize you make sure you pick up an odd number of cards, but younger children probably won't—and the trick works every time!

1 Spread the whole deck of cards out on a table and ask a member of the audience to come forward and select as many cards as she wants to, without actually looking at what she is doing. Once she's satisfied with her pile of cards, send her to one side of the stage area to count them.

2 While she is busy counting her cards, you also pick up a bunch of cards as casually as you can, but the secret is that *you always pick up an odd number of cards.*

3 Now tell your volunteer that whatever the number of cards she has—and *you don't want to know the number*—if she has an even number, the cards you have picked up will make them odd, and if she has an odd number, the cards you have picked up will make them even.

4 She now counts out the cards she has onto the table. You then pass your cards to her and ask her to count all the cards. The new total will, of course, be as you predicted.

5 There are two things to remember with this little trick. You need to practice casually scooping up an odd number of cards at will—ease with this will make the trick run even better. And you don't make fun of anyone—especially your volunteer—because it's so easy!

Trick 35
Unfair Deal

★ **You need:** a deck of cards, a table

Even though the cards for this trick are arranged while you—the magician—are not looking, you can still pick which card was selected. That's magic!

1 Before the performance, put all the 4s at the top of the deck and all the 9s at the bottom of the deck. Practice shuffling so these eight cards stay right where they are.

All the 4s

All the 9s

2 In front of your audience, shuffle the cards as described above. Fan them facedown and ask a volunteer to select one card from the deck. While your volunteer shows the card to the rest of the audience (but not you), close the deck and deal the cards into four equal piles by laying them one, one, one, one and two, two, two, two, rather than a pile at a time. (One pile will have one card fewer than the others.)

3 Now turn your back on the cards and the table, and ask your volunteer to place his chosen card on one of the piles. He then stacks the piles in any order he likes and hands the whole deck back to you.

4 You begin to fan out the whole deck and immediately pull the selected card from the fanned cards. How did you do it? Well, the secret is that once the cards are dealt into four piles, there will be a 4 on the bottom of each pile and a 9 on the top of each. When you fan out the cards, the selected card will be the card that is between a 4 and a 9.

5 You don't have to use 4s and 9s; you can use any numbers you want, but stay clear of the face cards. When several face cards lie next to each other, it is easier to see the trick.

Trick 36
Sticky Hands

★ **You need:** a deck of cards, a ring, a toothpick, a table

This is another easy trick for young (and old!) magicians. It's easy to learn, easy to perform, and easy to make look good!

1 To get ready for this trick, put on the ring. Now turn your palm so it's facing up. Slide the toothpick into the ring.

2 Place your hand carefully down on the table, making sure the audience doesn't see the toothpick. Your patter needs to include telling the audience you

are about to magically lift several playing cards with just the palm of your hand. You won't be holding on to them; they will just magically rise as you lift your hand.

3 Take a card with your other hand and slide it under the hand on the table, making sure one end of the card slides under the toothpick.

Diabolically Clever Card Tricks

4 Pick up another card and slide it under your hand from the other direction; this time you want it between your hand and the other end of the toothpick.

5 Try putting another four cards under your hand now; they will be held in place by the original two cards.

6 Say your favorite magic phrase—such as "Abracadabra" or "Sim Sala Bim"—and slowly lift your hand with the cards horizontally above the table. The cards will stay with your hand—it's magic!

Trick 37
Gone! Into Thin Air

★ **You need:** a deck of cards, a handkerchief with a hem, a toothpick, scissors, a table

So you've dazzled the audience by finding the cards they've picked, but how about making cards disappear? That would be fun...

1 A little bit of preparation for this trick is necessary. Make sure the toothpick is as long as the width of a playing card—if it's too long, trim it. Now poke this toothpick into the hem of the handkerchief. You're ready for an audience!

2 Begin with a flourish by spreading the deck of cards on the table. Wave the handkerchief about and tell your audience you'll pick a card from the deck and make it vanish into thin air.

3 Lay the handkerchief over the cards so the edge with the toothpick is folded under the handkerchief.

TOOTHPICK

MAGIC TRICKS

4 Pick up the edge of the handkerchief that contains the toothpick by holding the toothpick between your thumb and index finger—it looks as if you are holding a card, right?

5 Say your favorite magic words, including something about making the card disappear. Throw the handkerchief into the air—the card appears to have vanished!

TRUE MAGIC! LOOK at that! NO CARD!

Cunning Coin Conundrums

Coins are easy to find around the home, so they are perfect for the budding magician to use in tricks. Of course, there are trick coins—double-headed and specialty—available at magic shops, but for most of the following tricks any coin will do!

Trick 38
Sleight of Hand

★ **You need:** one coin

All magicians learn sleight of hand. Learn this trick well and you can perform it at any time in any place: a show, a party, or even a restaurant!

From the other side... Can't see the coin

1 Begin by placing the coin firmly between the first knuckles of the index and middle fingers of one hand. The coin should be hidden, so that when you present your open hand (palm out) to the audience, they can't see a thing.

2 Now we come to the part that you need to practice and practice. To produce the coin, you turn your fingers in toward the palm of your hand and use your thumb to flip the coin upward.

Juliet... Here art thou Romeo...

You're no Magician!!

GET OFF!

We want MAGIC!

Did you know?
By the 1800s, magic was often performed in theaters in many countries. At some venues, magicians performed regularly.

Trick 39
Spin That Coin

★ **You need:** a quarter or dime, two pins, a table

This is so simple, it's not really a trick. In fact, anyone can do it, but you're the one who has practiced and practiced to make sure it works every time!

1 Place the coin on the table and pick it up gently between the points of the pins.

2 Once you're sure it's secure, blow really gently on the coin, and it will begin to spin.

3 That's all there is to it! It's a great trick to open a small magic show. You only need to keep the coin spinning for a few seconds—or longer if you like—to ensure that the audience thinks you're a great magician!

Trick 40
Where's My Coin?

★ **You need:** a ball of yarn, a special coin slide, a coin, a glass, a table

It's time to make a coin disappear, then reappear! A bit of preparation is needed for this trick—you need to make a metal slide to ensure the coin reaches the inside of the ball of yarn—otherwise no trick!

1 Before your audience arrives, wind a fairly loose ball of yarn and prepare the metal slide—it can be a flat piece of tin or a small, but wide, metal ruler. Make sure the metal slide can slip easily into the ball of yarn. You will use it to put the coin inside the yarn. Place both props on your table, but out of sight of your audience. The slide should be inserted partway into the ball of yarn.

2 Borrow a coin from an audience member. (You should have a coin on hand in case no one has one!) Hold it carefully between the tips of the thumb and index finger of your left hand.

3 Bring your right hand over your left hand as if to take the coin, but as soon as your right hand shields the coin from the audience's sight, let the coin drop into the palm of your left hand.

MAGIC TRICKS

4 As the coin drops, close your right hand into a fist—as if you are holding the coin—and move it away to the right, making sure you follow your right hand with your eyes, so the audience will look there, too. As you do this, just let your left hand fall down to your side quite normally.

5 While you are doing all this, of course, you are chatting to your audience. Talk about how quickly money disappears these days—here one minute, gone the next. As you get to this part of your patter, open your right hand slowly and appear astonished that the coin has vanished.

6 At the same time, reach for the ball of yarn with your left hand and drop the coin into the slide. Push the coin into the ball of yarn, then pull the slide free. It sounds like a lot to do while you are continuing to chat to your audience about how money seems to vanish so quickly, but with lots of practice you'll be amazed at how good this part of the trick can look!

7 Now show the audience the ball of yarn, place it in the glass, and unravel it gently. The coin will clink into the glass. Now, hand the coin back to the person you borrowed it from and ask if it's the same coin. Of course, it is, and everyone's impressed!

Trick 41
The Coin Fold

★ **You need:** a coin, a small piece of paper

Another easy but effective trick using just one coin—especially suitable for a small audience.

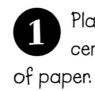

1 Place the coin in the center of the piece of paper.

2 Fold the bottom edge of the paper up and over the coin, leaving a .25-in. (6-mm) gap between the two edges of the paper.

3 Fold the right edge of the paper back behind the coin.

4 Then fold the left edge of the paper back behind the coin.

MAGIC TRICKS

5 Make the final fold by bending the top flap of the paper back behind the coin. It seems as if the coin is completely wrapped, but in fact the top edge is still open.

6 You now turn the package around so the open edge allows the coin to slip into the palm of your hand, where it stays while you "prove" the coin has disappeared by tearing up the paper package.

WOOPS!

Did you know?
Harry Houdini (Ehrich Weiss was his real name) is still the best-known magician. He was known as an escapologist, and his motto was "No Jail Could Hold Him!" He often performed outdoors, too, which added to the drama. He escaped from a straitjacket while hanging by his ankles tied high above a street—he received plenty of publicity for that trick!

Trick 42
Now You See It, Now You Don't!

> ★ **You need:** two sheets of same-colored paper, one sheet of paper in another color, a glass, glue, scissors, a coin, a wand (optional)

Actually the saying needs to be reversed for this disappearing and reappearing coin. Read on!

1 Before the show begins, make a magic cone from the single sheet of colored paper. Secure it with glue and add stars and glitter to make it look magical.

2 Next, cut a circle from one of the other sheets of paper using the glass as your guide, and glue it to the rim of the glass. This will cover the coin and will not be seen, as it will be resting on a sheet of same-colored paper. Put the magic cone, glass, and coin on the remaining sheet of paper. (The glass should be upside down.) Now you're ready for your audience.

GLUE

PAPER

PAPER GLUED ON

87

MAGIC TRICKS

 3 Tell your audience the cone is endowed with magic powers and can make things disappear. You will make the coin disappear.

4 Cover the glass with the cone and place both over the coin. Tap the cone with a wand or simply wave your hands while saying magic words, such as "Abracadabra!"

5 Lift up the cone to show the glass, but no coin—it has been magically spirited away.

6 Of course, the coin is really still on the table, but the paper on the rim of the glass is covering the coin. Therefore, it's easy for you to be a really clever magician and restore the coin to the table by reversing the process. Place the cone over the glass again, use a few simple magic words

and a flourish of hands, and pick up the cone and the glass. There it is—the coin has reappeared!

> I HAVEN'T GOT TIME FOR MAGIC I'M TOO BUSY DRIVING ROUND THE UNIVERSE!

Did you know?

Popular magicians took their traveling shows around the world. Early in the twentieth century, one American magician had his Wonder Show of the Universe touring the world. He was America's top performer for 30 years.

 Cunning Coin Conundrums

CHAPTER 3

Trick 43
Where's That Coin?

★ **You need:** a handkerchief, a coin, poster putty, a table

In this trick, a coin is placed in the center of a handkerchief in full view of an audience—the magician weaves a magic spell, and it's gone!

1 Before facing your audience, stick a small piece of poster putty to one corner of the handkerchief. This needs to be kept hidden from the audience at all times during the performance.

2 Spread the handkerchief out on the table, keeping hold of the corner that has the poster putty. Place the coin in the center of the handkerchief and immediately cover it with the corner with the poster putty.

CORNER WITH POSTER PUTTY

MAGIC TRICKS

3 Fold the other three corners into the center of the handkerchief over the coin.

4 Place the fingers of both of your hands under the folded edge of the handkerchief that is nearest you. Because of this quick move, the coin, stuck to the handkerchief, ends up in your hand.

5 Show both sides of the handkerchief to the audience, give it a quick shake and put it in your pocket to finish. Pretend to blow your nose on it, or pretend to sneeze and cover your nose and mouth with it—anything for a good finale and a round of applause!

6 Perhaps you would like to make this coin reappear? It can be done—of course it can—it's magic! Or it's good planning. Simply have an identical coin hidden somewhere strange—down the top of your sock maybe. Or when you remove the coin from the handkerchief, keep it in your hand and then produce it from anywhere you like—maybe from behind the ear of one of your audience members?

Great... I need a hankie to blow my nose!

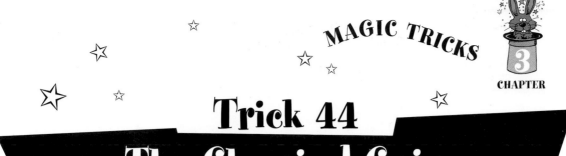

Trick 44
The Chemical Coin

★ **You need:** one coin, a table, a chair

You'll also need some good patter. It's best to perform this intriguing trick before a small audience.

1 Your story should begin as soon as the audience arrives. Talk excitedly about what you've just read on the internet—that chemicals in the human body can break down the metals that make up a coin. In fact, coins can just disappear!

2 Show the coin to your audience and sit down at your table resting your chin on your right hand. Begin rubbing the coin held in your left hand against your right forearm, making sure no one can actually see the coin as you do this.

3 While you are rubbing the coin on your arm, continue telling the fantastic story you began your show with. Now the coin should slip out of your left hand and drop on to the table. Continue with the story and make sure you are looking at your audience.

MAGIC TRICKS

4 Pick up the dropped coin in your right hand and pretend to pass it back into your left hand, but actually keep it in your right hand.

5 Prop up your chin again in your right hand and pretend to rub the coin on your forearm as before. This movement must be done really masterfully and you must continue telling your story while this happens.

6 Keep on rubbing for a little longer, then suddenly look a little concerned. Continue to rub— maybe even a bit harder—and then slowly stop the rubbing, lifting your left hand fingers one at a time.

At the same time, you carefully drop the coin into your shirt collar. Then, with a flourish, show your audience the coin has disappeared, just as you predicted!

Trick 45
Holey Napkin

★ **You need:** a coin, a cloth napkin, a black marker

This is a very impressive trick—easy to do and great to watch!

1 Your audience must be seated directly in front of you, as with most tricks! Ask a volunteer for a coin or hand over yours and ask the volunteer to label it with the marker so it will be recognizable later on.

2 Hold the coin upright between the thumb and index finger of your left hand.

3 Place the napkin over the top, so that the coin is in the center of the cloth.

MAGIC TRICKS

4 Now for the tricky bit. Carefully arrange a small fold of the napkin between your thumb and the coin. With your right hand, lift the front of the napkin and drape it back over the top of the napkin and over your left wrist.

COIN
FOLD

5 Make a point of showing your audience the coin is still there.

COIN

6 Continue to hold both the coin and the napkin. Then flick your left wrist forward, which will make both halves of the napkin fall forward.

7 Now twist the napkin so it appears the coin is wrapped securely inside it. Squeeze the edge of the coin a little, and it should rise magically up through the napkin—or that is how it will appear to your audience!

Trick 46
The Coin Tells

★ **You need:** four coins of different values, a table

You'll be amazed at how simple this trick is—don't forget to learn some good patter to ensure your audience is really convinced it's magic!

1 Place the four coins on the table while talking about telepathy. Ask an audience member to choose a coin while your back is turned. Tell her to hold it tightly and concentrate hard so you can pick up the vibes from her mind!

2 Concentrate silently for a few moments, pretending you are trying to pick up thought waves—but what you're really doing is slowly counting to 30.

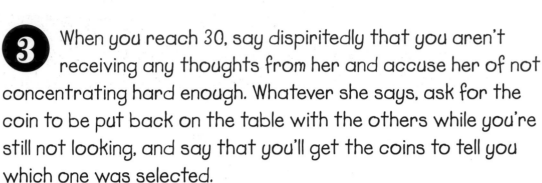

MAGIC TRICKS

3 When you reach 30, say dispiritedly that you aren't receiving any thoughts from her and accuse her of not concentrating hard enough. Whatever she says, ask for the coin to be put back on the table with the others while you're still not looking, and say that you'll get the coins to tell you which one was selected.

4 Turn around and pick up each coin in turn and hold it up to your ear to "hear" it "talking" to you. What you're really doing is feeling each coin, because the one that has been held by your volunteer will be much warmer than the others.

5 Once you find the warmest coin, show it to the audience and wait for the applause!

I HEARD THIS ONE SAY...
IT'S ME... IT'S ME!

Trick 47
The Weeping Coin

> ★ **You need:** a coin, a small piece of wet (but not dripping) sponge

An emotional, crying coin? What next!?

SPONGE

1 Before your audience arrives, wet the piece of sponge and make sure it fits between the coin and your thumb without being seen by the audience. It must hold enough water to allow you to make the coin "cry" tears.

2 Once the audience is there, hold up the coin between your thumb and index finger (keeping the wet sponge hidden with your thumb), and tell them a really good story about how some coins are very emotional and you bet you can get this one to cry!

3 Now squeeze the sponge gently while you yell at the coin. Tears should begin to flow!

OH...! WHAT A SAD LITTLE COIN! DID I MAKE YOU CRY?

4 Once the tears stop, put the sponge and coin in your pocket. If a member of the audience wants to check the coin is real, just pull it out again—minus the sponge, of course.

MAGIC TRICKS

Trick 48
Snatch!

★ **You need:** a coin

Again, a simple coin trick that makes the magician look very, very clever! The idea is to put a coin in the palm of your hand and challenge a volunteer to snatch it from you before you can close your hand. Your volunteer can't do it, but when you switch places, you get the coin on your first try.

 1 Put the coin on your palm and keep it flat. Have your volunteer hold his hand above yours.

 2 Your volunteer now tries to grab the coin before you close your hand—be as quick as you can. Your volunteer will fail every time.

 3 Now swap.

 4 How do you do it? Place your fingers and thumb together, without touching, and make sure these fingers are pointing down toward the coin.

 5 Quickly move your hand down, gently striking the palm of your volunteer's hand with your fingertips. This action means the volunteer's hand will be pushed downward a little, and the coin will jump up into your waiting fingers! Try it! It works!

Classic Conjuring

Every magician needs to spend some time perfecting a few classic magic tricks. Don't worry if some of the tricks seem old-fashioned or so well-known you think everyone will know how they're done; it's what you say and how you perform them that your friends will love. You'll probably think of a new way to do one or more of them anyway. That's OK—magic doesn't stay the same.

MAGIC TRICKS

Trick 49
Long Arm

★ **You need:** your arm, a jacket or coat

Perhaps not a classic trick, but a classic effect. People love seeing a magician do something they don't think they can do themselves.

1 You'll need to practice this trick over and over again— try doing it in front of a mirror so you can see the effect you are trying to create. You do need to wear a jacket or a coat while performing (and practicing) this trick.

2 First, stand still and bend your arm so your left hand and wrist are level with your waist.

3 Now, with the other hand, pinch the loose skin on the back of your left hand near the knuckle of the middle finger.

4 Shake this skin loose a little. As you do, it appears you're actually stretching your arm by tugging it out of its sleeve to an abnormal length. That's all there is to this trick, but it's so effective when done really well and with a great story. For example, you could make up a tale about a trip to Longreach, Australia (a real place!).

PRESS SLEEVE AGAINST YOU HERE

5 Once you've pulled out the really long arm, you can tap your arm back inside the jacket sleeve as part of the story.

6 The effect is created by hugging the jacket or coat sleeve tightly to your body as you move your arm a normal length. Don't let the audience see your elbow just above the hem of the sleeve or you'll give the trick away!

MAGIC TRICKS

Trick 50
Where's My Thumb?

★ **You need:** just your hands

This trick takes much longer to read about than to do! But you'll need to practice for several weeks before you'll be ready to perform it. You want your audience to believe the tip of your left thumb is being magically removed—without any blood!—from your hand.

1 How do you do this? Begin by holding your left hand in front of you, at about waist height. The palm of your hand faces toward you; your fingers are flat and pointing to the right. Make sure your thumb is parallel to your index finger.

2 Pretend to pull the tip off your left thumb with your right thumb and index finger. Make a big deal of this with lots of grunts and groans and twisted facial expressions! Of course you can't do it, can you?

3 Well maybe you can! Try again, and this time, as you place your right index finger over the left thumb joint, bend the top of your left thumb down and put your right thumb so it looks as if it has replaced it.

4 Well, if you thought that was difficult, wait until you try this part! Tuck the other fingers of the right hand away so the audience can clearly see your right thumb tip—which, of course now looks as if it is your left thumb tip! Got it? Good!

5 To complete the illusion, keep your left hand still and slowly slide the right thumb along the top of your left index finger. Then slowly slide it back to the original spot.

6 When your thumbs touch, show your hands with thumbs intact to your audience! Take a bow!

Trick 51
Silky Hankie

★ **You need:** a small flesh-colored rubber band, a large patterned silk square, a ring, a table

This is a simple trick you can do practically anywhere–great for entertaining young children and adults alike! Show them you can make a ring disappear!

1 Before facing your audience, slip a rubber band over three of the fingers on your left hand.

2 Once your audience arrives, take out your silk hankie and wave it about using your right hand so all eyes are on it and not on the rubber band over your fingers! You don't want your audience to notice the rubber band.

3 Spread the hankie over your left hand with a flourish and secretly slip your thumb into the rubber band to widen it a little more.

4 Ask your audience if you can borrow a ring. (Of course, if they haven't got one, you already happen to have one on your table!)

5 Show everyone the ring and then place it on the silk hankie above the rubber band. With your free hand, rub the ring saying a magic chant. Of course, what you are doing is pushing the ring through the band into a fold of silk below.

RUBBER BAND

RING PUSHED DOWN INTO FOLD

6 Slip the band off your fingers to trap the ring in a fold in the silk while making a dramatic gesture and saying more magic words.

7 Dramatically whip the hankie away with your right hand and look amazed to see that the ring has disappeared from your left hand.

RING IN FOLD

8 Return the ring by spreading the silk over your left hand again; reach into the folds with your right hand and pull out the ring with a smile!

MAGIC TRICKS

Trick 52
Pass-Through Hand

★ **You need:** your hands, a coin

This trick will entertain everyone when you perform it smoothly and with lots of great acting!

1 Make a fist with your left hand and hold the coin above it in your right hand.

2 Tell your audience that you intend to push the coin right through your hand. Begin pushing the coin down between the fingers of your left hand.

3 As it goes, it will slide out of sight behind your fingers, so you can proudly announce that it's "gone through" your hand.

COIN PUSHED IN BETWEEN FINGERS

4 You open your fist, but there is no coin, so you have to pretend you think it's stuck halfway! Ask your audience where they think it is—there will nearly always be people who think they know!

5 Try again, and this time add the tricky bit. As you turn your left hand back over into a fist, your thumb nearly touches the fingers holding the coin. Just as this happens, let the coin slip down from your fingers into your left hand at the same time as you make it into a fist again.

6 Because you've practiced and practiced, it all goes smoothly. The audience will tell you they think the coin is still hidden by your fingers somehow. Say you'll push harder this time, and then slowly turn your fist and open it up to reveal the coin!

MAGIC TRICKS

Trick 53
The Classic Scarf Trick

★ **You need:** a long silky scarf, a high-necked top

Most of the classic tricks are very simple, just like this one. The real trick for a magician—young or old—is to be smooth and professional!

1 Prepare for this trick by tucking the silky scarf into the neck of your high-necked top at the front and sides only.

2 In front of your audience, hold the ends of the scarf securely and pull both ends forward on the count of three, or perhaps while chanting "Sim Sala Bim!"

3 To complete the illusion, pull the scarf forward in one quick motion so it appears to pass straight through your neck! Wait for the applause!

Look... you can handcuff me, dangle me over icy rivers in a straitjacket... lock me in a cell and throw away the key. ...BUT PLEASE DON'T HIT ME IN THE TUMMY!

Did you know?

Harry Houdini died in agony after a student, who had heard he could withstand a powerful blow to the belly, punched Houdini before he was ready. He was taken to the hospital and died a few days later.

Trick 54
The Magic Cone

★ **You need:** a paper cone with a secret pocket, a silk hankie

It's worth finding a special cone, or making your own for this trick, as it's likely to be one of the best tricks you do. Tell your audience you will make a silk hankie disappear.

SECRET POCKET

1 Unfold the cone so your audience can see it's just a cone with one decorated side and one plain side. (We know better!)

SECRET POCKET

2 Fold it back into a cone shape and push the silk hankie into the secret pocket. To the audience, it should look as if you're just pushing the hankie into the cone.

3 Speak some magic words and clap your hands together, flattening the cone and the hankie in the pocket!

4 Unfold the cone carefully and show that there is nothing on the front or back of it—the hankie has gone!

Trick 55
How Eggstraordinary!

★ **You need:** an egg, a silk hankie, a pencil, a teaspoon, an egg cup (optional)

Done well, with lots of clever patter, this trick will make your audience believe you can pull a hankie out of an egg.

1 First, carefully prepare the egg. Make a hole in the side of an uncooked egg. Gently drain the contents of the egg and save them to eat later. Wash the shell inside and let it sit and dry naturally. Once the shell has dried, carefully poke your silk hankie into the hole with a pencil.

HOLE AT BACK

2 Now you need to convince your audience you have lost your hankie, but you're going to eat an egg instead. Of course, they will think it's a boiled egg, so when you hold it up in the air for the audience to see—keeping the hole toward you—you could pretend it's hot.

MAGIC TRICKS

3 Now, pop the egg back on the table and tap it gently with your spoon, then gasp and say something like: "How 'eggstraordinary!' You'll never guess where I've found my hankie."

4 Break the egg apart excitedly, pull out the hankie, and wave it in the air.

OH GREAT...! There's supposed to be a rabbit in this hat to make disappear... But it's already... DISAPPEARED!

Classic Conjuring

Trick 56
How Many Balls?

★ **You need: three small sponge balls**

To do this trick, you'll need to learn a new skill—it's called palming.

1 First, you need to learn to palm the sponge balls—at least they aren't very large! Place one ball in the palm of your hand. Bring your thumb over a little way to hold it in position; it shouldn't move, even when you hold your hand upright. Practice until you can keep the sponge ball in place when you are moving your hands around a lot. Now try to palm two balls!

2 Once you are really good at palming, you're ready to move on to the next step, which is tricking an audience.

3 Have all three balls in your pocket before you begin your performance. Tell the audience you are getting two balls out of your pocket. Show the audience the two balls in your right hand.

MAGIC TRICKS

You have also palmed a ball, so there are really three balls in your right hand, but the audience must see only two of them.

4 Tell the audience you are moving one ball to your left hand. While you move the ball, secretly move the third ball to your left hand, too.

5 Now hold two balls up in the air, one in each hand, and ask your audience to agree that you have one ball in each hand. They, of course, will agree, and then you pass the ball from your right hand to your left hand, saying as you do: "Of course, now I have two balls in my left hand, don't I?"

6 But, of course, you don't—there are three balls nestling in your hand.

7 Palming will come in very handy throughout your magic career—learn to do it well!

OF COURSE IT'S A REAL GRENADE... EVERYTHING IS **REAL** IN MAGIC!

Did you know?
During the *Second World War, many* magicians entertained the troops. Magicians traveled overseas as well as performing on home ground.

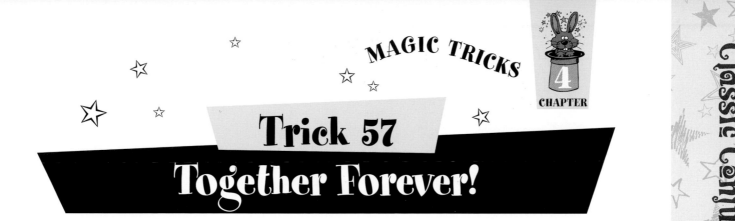

Trick 57
Together Forever!

★ **You need:** one bill of paper money, two paperclips

This is another simple trick. Tell your audience you can make two paperclips link up without touching them.

1 Stand directly in front of your audience and fold the five dollar bill into a Z shape. Place the paperclips on the folded bill as shown in the picture.

2 Hold up the bill so the audience can see what it looks like, then warn the front row of the audience they may have to duck!

3 Now carefully hold the bill at each end and quickly snap it back into a straightened position. The paper clips will link themselves together and possibly fly right out into the audience!

4 Stand by for loud applause.

Trick 58
The Spinning Egg

★ **You need:** eleven fresh eggs, one hard-boiled egg, a table

Whatever you do, don't drop any of the fresh eggs!

1 Prepare for this trick by hard-boiling an egg. And then, when the egg cools, place it back in the egg carton with the fresh eggs—making sure you remember its position.

2 Once you are in front of your audience, pass out the eggs to eleven volunteers, keeping the hard-boiled one for yourself.

3 Using your egg (which no-one but you knows is hard-boiled), show the volunteers how to spin an egg. Obviously you need to practice first!

4 Then invite your eleven volunteers up one by one to try to spin their eggs. No one will be able to do this little trick because a fresh egg won't spin.

5 Actually, it's even more fun if there are two hard-boiled eggs in the carton, because then one of the volunteers really will be able to spin an egg and you can make a big deal out of it!

Trick 59
Cups and Balls

> ★ **You need:** three cups, four small sponge balls, one larger sponge ball

This may be the oldest magic trick—hiding a ball under a cup! Magicians all over the world learn it to entertain and confuse their audiences.

The special cups used in this trick can be purchased wherever magic props are sold; consider buying a set of clear plastic cups to begin with, so you can see exactly where each ball is as you learn. Each cup has a rim that prevents another cup from being pushed completely inside it, enabling a ball to be hidden in the space created. Also, the bottom of each cup has an indentation that, when the cup is upside down, lets a soft sponge ball rest on it without rolling.

1 To prepare, place the large ball in your left pocket, one small ball in each of the three cups, and the fourth small ball in your left hand. Place the cups inside each other. They should be sitting mouth-up.

MAGIC TRICKS

2 When you begin the performance, turn each cup over quickly, keeping the ball hidden underneath.

3 Tap or wave your hand over all the cups and then lift the right one with your right hand to reveal a ball resting on the table underneath it. Transfer the cup to your left hand, so it covers the small ball hidden there.

4 Repeat with the other two cups, showing the two other balls, and placing the cups over the one already in your left hand.

5 Now place each cup mouth-down directly behind a ball on the table. Place the last cup you lifted behind the right ball. Place the second cup you lifted behind the left ball. Place the first cup you lifted behind the center ball. As you place this cup on the table, make sure the concealed ball drops into it before you turn it mouth-down.

6 Pick up the center ball and place it on top of the center cup. Next, place both the other cups on top of the ball. With a tap or wave of your hand, lift all three cups as one to reveal a ball on the table. To the audience, it appears as though you have magically made the ball pass through the base of the cup. Wait for the applause... and then say: "But wait, there's more!"

7 Hold the stack of cups mouth-up so the hidden ball is now resting inside the middle cup. Separate the cups again and place the empty ones mouth-down on the table, behind the right and left balls. Put the cup with the ball mouth-down over the center ball. Place a ball on top of this cup and repeat step 6, inviting a volunteer to tap the cup. While your volunteer is doing this, take the large ball from your pocket and hold it in your left hand.

8 When you lift the stack of cups again, astonishingly, three small balls are on the table. Casually place the cups mouth-down in your left hand and act as though the trick is finished by placing the stack of cups mouth-down on the table.

9 A bit of acting here will earn you enormous applause, so hesitate as if you want to tell your audience something, but shouldn't. Then say you'll reveal a magic secret: You did use more than three balls for the trick! Pick up the cups to reveal a much larger ball—to more applause!

THANK YOU!
THANK YOU!
THANK YOU!

Masterly Mental Magic

A magician can gain much by learning a few mentally challenging tricks. They always work and will make the magician look, well, magical! Many are card tricks, many need a little bit of preparation, and, of course, they all need practice—but it's worth the trouble, as they are all terrific tricks to perform.

Trick 60
Clever Colors

★ **You need:** six index cards, a black marker, a table

Keeping the audience's attention on the great names of colors you have chosen will distract them from the simplicity of this trick!

1 A little preparation is necessary for this trick. Write the name of a different color on each index card. Be creative with the names of the colors because you need a different number of letters for each color. Perhaps you'll choose red (3), blue (4), green (5), yellow (6), magenta (7), and lavender (8).

MAGIC TRICKS

2 Now you're ready for your audience. Place the cards randomly on a table with the names of the colors facing up, and ask a volunteer to pick a color.

3 Your volunteer is not to tell anyone the name of the color, but must silently spell the name of the color, one letter at a time, as you touch each card. When your volunteer reaches the last letter of the color, he must say "Stop," and your hand will be resting on the correct card!

4 How does it work? Well, for the first two letters you touch any cards you want; then you touch the three-letter color, the four-letter color, and so on. You will always be on the correct card when the volunteer tells you to stop!

Trick 61
Wacky Clock

★ **You need:** a large photocopy of a clock face, a pencil

Find a really great clock face to photocopy, because the more zany it is, the more it will distract your audience from the simple, but clever, trick you are about to do for them.

1 Ask a volunteer to look at the photocopied clock face and select a number from it—silently! Ask your volunteer to add 1 to the number she selects; so if she chooses 7, she adds 1 to make 8, keeping all this in her head.

2 If she needs to write down the number she first thought of, let her do so, but make sure you can't see it.

3 Now for the clever bit! Ask your volunteer to begin counting silently from the number she now has (in our example, the volunteer starts with 9) each time you tap your pencil on the clock's face.

4 When she gets to 20, she is to say "Stop!" Remarkably, you will be on the correct number, so you circle it on the clock's face and hand it to your volunteer facedown. She is to tell the audience the number she originally selected and then turn over the photocopy to reveal your answer. Your answer will be correct every time!

COUNTERCLOCKWISE FROM 6

5 The secret? You begin tapping on the clock's face at the number 6 each time you do the trick and you tap counterclockwise on the numbers. When your volunteer says "stop" at 20, you will always be on the correct number.

6 If you are going to repeat this trick in front of the same audience, make sure no one sees where you begin tapping each time.

Trick 62
Plus and Minus

★ **You need:** a piece of paper, a pencil

This is an easy one if your math skills are good. You can't use a calculator—it just doesn't look as impressive!

1 Ask a member of your audience to write a five-digit number on the piece of paper. The number must be made up of five different digits, and the first digit must be a larger number than the last. Your volunteer keeps this piece of paper and his math work hidden from you at all times. Let's say he chooses 36412.

2 Now ask him to reverse the number, write it underneath the first number, and subtract the second from the first number. In our example, the answer is 14949.

3 Now ask your volunteer to reverse this answer, write the reverse underneath it, and add the two numbers.

MAGIC TRICKS

4 Once he says he has an answer, you as the magician must act up a storm, saying you can read his mind and know the number he has arrived at. It will always be 109890 or 99099. If you are wrong on the first guess, just blame bad vibes and say, "Ah, it's coming to me now…!"

Trick 63
Famous Names

★ **You need:** ten cards big enough to write names on but small enough to fit into the magic hat, a pencil, a piece of paper, a hat

You'll choose the correct name every time, but you can only do this trick once per audience!

1 Ask people in your audience to call out ten famous names. As they do, write each name on a card and place it in the hat. Well, that's what *your* audience thinks you're doing! What you are really doing is repeatedly writing down the first name called; perhaps it was Nelson Mandela. Write that on a card, place it in the hat, and pretend to write down the next nine names called out. Maybe you'll hear Madonna, Tom Cruise, Shakespeare, and others shouted out— but every time you write down Nelson Mandela and put the card in the hat!

MAGIC TRICKS

2 Now, of course, it's easy. You ask someone from the audience to come up and pick a name out of the hat and read it, but not tell anyone.

3 You ask your volunteer to concentrate hard on the name and you do the same, making sure you act as if it is very hard to do! After a few seconds of this, tell the audience you now believe you can read the volunteer's mind, and the answer is "Nelson Mandela."

4 Everyone will be astounded and will cheer and clap wildly. On no account are you to repeat this trick with the same audience—for obvious reasons!

Trick 64
Mystery Math

★ **You need:** a piece of paper, a pencil

Astonish your audience with your quick-as-lightning number skills.

1 Ask an audience member to call out a single-digit number. (Let's say it's 3.) Ask another audience member to call out any single-digit number. (Let's say it's 4.)

2 Without hesitating, write on the piece of paper the number that you predict will come up at the end of this trick and show the number to the audience.

3 Now tell your audience to double the first number (3 x 2 = 6), add the second number (6 + 4 = 10), divide the answer by 2 (10 ÷ 2 = 5), and subtract the original number (5 – 3 = 2).

4 Your prediction was right, of course, and your audience thinks you're a genius!

5 How did you do it? It's easy—the final number is always half the adding number (the second number chosen by your audience). You can repeat this trick as many times as you want; it'll always work, and it's one that audiences rarely figure out, even though it's really simple!

Masterly Mental Magic

Trick 65
They Match!

★ **You need:** two pieces of paper, two pencils

This little trick won't fool your audience for long, but it's great for a laugh. You tell the audience that your powers of mental concentration are so good that you will be able to write the same sentence as someone from the audience.

1 Ask a volunteer to write a sentence on one of the pieces of paper—it can be anything your volunteer likes. Your volunteer then folds the paper and hands it to another member of the audience.

2 Put the other piece of paper in front of you and tell the audience you are going to write the same sentence. Pretend to be concentrating hard. Write down "You're right, they match!" on your piece of paper. Fold it and hand it to the same person who is holding the sentence written by the volunteer.

3 Ask this person to open the volunteer's piece of paper and read the sentence aloud.

4 Now ask this person to open the paper containing the sentence *you* wrote and read it aloud. The reader will laugh (of course!) and then say, "You're right, they match!" because that is what's written on the paper!

5 You audience will be tremendously amazed and clap and cheer, until the reader tells them the truth!

Trick 66
Secrets? What Secrets?

★ **You need: two pieces of paper, a pen or pencil**

People who use calculators to do their arithmetic may find this trick a bit hard. Your volunteer will need to calculate everything on paper unless you can find a calculator that has room for a nine-digit answer!

1 Begin by asking for a volunteer to help you with this trick.

2 Give him a piece of paper and a pen or pencil, and tell him he is going to do some silent calculations. Then, just by looking at the final answer, you, the magician, will be able to tell the volunteer's phone number and age!

3 First of all, the volunteer writes his phone number on the paper, then multiplies it by 2. (See the example.) Now ask him to do the following: add 5 to the total, then multiply it by 50, add his age, add 365, and finally subtract 615.

$$
\begin{array}{r}
2879192 \\
\times\ 2 \\
\hline
5758384 \\
\end{array}
$$

$$
\begin{array}{r}
5758384 \\
+\ 5 \\
\hline
5758389 \\
\end{array}
$$

$$5758389$$
$$\times 50$$
$$287919450$$

$$287919450$$
$$+ 49$$
$$287919499$$

$$287919499$$
$$+ 365$$
$$287919864$$

$$287919864$$
$$- 615$$
$$287919249$$

4 The last two numbers in the above sequence—49—represent the volunteer's age, and the first seven numbers are his phone number. Of course, if the second-to-last number is 0, the volunteer is under 10 years old, and only the last number represents his age.

5 This trick is very effective if you can remember the sequence of instructions without referring to a book or notes. And don't be persuaded to repeat this trick for the same group—once will leave them wondering.

You're going to have to move close to the screen to see this one. I'll turn this little FLEA into a DUST MITE!

Did you know?
After television was invented, people began to stay home more. Magicians wanting to perform successfully on this new medium had to create smaller, cleverer tricks.

133

MAGIC TRICKS

Trick 67
Supersweet Numbers

★ **You need:** a bowl of sugar cubes, a glass of water, a table, a pencil

Plenty of practice and good patter will help you perform this popular trick.

1 Place the bowl of sugar cubes and glass of water on the table in front of your audience. Have a volunteer choose a number between 1 and 10. With the pencil, write the number darkly on a sugar cube.

2 Show the cube to your audience. Then press it between your thumb and finger, with the number facing your thumb. The number will transfer onto your thumb as you press. Now drop the cube into the glass of water and let it dissolve.

PRESS THE NUMBER ONTO YOUR THUMB

PRESS NUMBER ONTO PALM

3 Hold your volunteer's hand over the glass. Say you're using your mental powers to make the number appear on her hand. Press your thumb into the palm of her hand. The number will transfer from your thumb to her palm.

4 Say, "Sim Sala Bim!" Then lift your volunteer's hand and show the number on her palm to the audience.

Trick 68
Dice Divination

★ **You need:** three dice, a pen, a piece of paper, a table

When performing this great trick, a smart magician must remember that the opposite sides of a die always add up to seven.

1 Use a lot of theatrics when performing this trick, because the trick really does itself. Show the audience the three dice, the pen, and the paper—and ask for a volunteer to help you.

2 While you stand at the back of the stage with your back to the audience, ask the volunteer to roll the three dice, pick them up in any order, and stack them one on top of the other.

3 Continue keeping your back to the audience and ask the volunteer to carefully add up the numbers of the five hidden faces of the dice. (See the illustration on the next page.) The volunteer now writes down this number and silently shows it to the audience.

MAGIC TRICKS

4 Once the audience has seen the paper with the number on it, the volunteer tear it up. Now you turn around and face the audience. Move to the table and stare at the stacked dice.

5 Bring your hands to your head, pretend that you are concentrating, and announce the correct answer to wild applause!

6 The secret to this trick is that the opposite sides of a die always add up to seven. You have three dice, so 7 multiplied by 3 equals 21. When you turn and step forward, you look at the number on the top die; let's say it is 5. Subtract 5 from 21 and you get 16. Tell your audience that 16 is the number on the piece of paper—and you'll be absolutely correct.

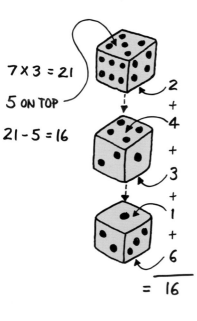

$7 \times 3 = 21$

5 ON TOP

$21 - 5 = 16$

2
+
4
+
3
+
1
+
6
= 16

7 Standing with your back to the audience, having the volunteer tear up the paper, and acting as if you were struggling with the answer just add drama—the answer is always right in front of you!

Trick 69
Magic Dates

★ **You need:** a pen, two pieces of paper, an envelope, a calculator (optional)

This simple but intriguing trick only requires the magician to know what year it is!

1 Write a number on one piece of paper and place it in the envelope. (Your audience will think it's a random choice, but you'll always double the current year. So if it's 2012, you'll write 4024.) Seal the envelope and ask for a volunteer.

2 When the volunteer comes forward, give him the sealed envelope and ask him to keep it in his pocket until you ask for it.

3 Give the volunteer the paper and pen and ask him to write down, then add up, the following four numbers:

      ◎   the year he was born

      ◎   the year he began school

      ◎   the age he'll be at the end of this year

      ◎   the number of years since he started school.

MAGIC TRICKS

4 For example, the numbers might look like this:

$$
\begin{array}{r}
2004 \\
2010 \\
8 \\
+\ 2 \\
\hline
4024
\end{array}
$$

5 When the volunteer has finished the addition, ask him to open the envelope. He will be astonished to find that you have already written the same answer and sealed it in the envelope!

6 If you want to ask an adult volunteer some questions, replace "the year he or she began school" and "the number of years since he or she started school" with either "the year he or she began working" and "the number of years since he or she began working" or "the year he or she got married" and "the number of years since he or she got married". The answer will always be the same—double the current year.

Trick 70
Old Timers' Card Trick

★ **You need:** a deck of cards

This is a trick that works itself, so you need to keep up the entertaining patter. Practice telling your story before unleashing this on your audience.

 Take any three cards from a full deck of cards, so you now have 49 cards in your hand.

 Ask a member of the audience to come forward and select any card from the deck, memorize it, put it back in the deck,

and then shuffle the deck thoroughly. Now, holding the cards facedown, ask your volunteer to deal the cards into seven faceup overlapping rows, dealing across the rows each time.

3 Stand well away as the volunteer does this, then ask the volunteer to search until she finds the card she memorized. Numbering the columns from left to right, ask her to tell you the number of the column her card is in. Ask her to close up the columns and stack the piles on top of each other. She should put the second pile on top of the first, the third on top of both, the fourth on top again, and so on.

MAGIC TRICKS

4 When all the piles are stacked, ask your volunteer to turn the stack facedown and deal the cards in the same way as before. Now request the number of the column containing the selected card. Mention that you have seen magicians who ask their volunteers to repeat this part of the trick over and over, but you can see that your volunteer is tiring, so twice will be enough.

5 Ask the volunteer to pile up the cards as before (second pile upon first, third upon second, and so on), and then ask her to start dealing them out one last time. After a while, stop her and say the next card will be the one she chose. And it will be!

6 How is this so? Well, the secret is simple mathematics—there is a formula that lets you "predict" the correct card every time! You subtract 1 from the second reported pile number and multiply this number by 7. Add on the first reported pile number, and the total gives the position of the card on the third deal.

7 So, if the card was in pile five the first time and pile one the second time, the formula would be: $1 - 1 = 0$; $0 \times 7 = 0$; $0 + 5 = 5$; so the fifth card dealt out in the third round will be the chosen card. Often it will be a card in the 20s or 30s that you are waiting for, so it might be a good idea to practice looking impatient!

Trick 71
Book Test

★ **You need:** a paperback book about 180-200 pages long, a playing card or a business card

This trick relies on *you* making it look as if *you* are doing one thing when *you* are actually doing another!

1 Either hand *your* own book to an audience member or ask to borrow a paperback book—a borrowed book will make *your* magical skills seem even greater!

2 Ask the audience member to flick through the pages to check that each page is different and that the book is genuine and has not been tampered with in any way.

3 Give him the playing card or business card and ask him to turn to any page in the book. Now ask him to look at the page number and the last word on that page and to concentrate hard on them. You should watch and see if he is looking at a right or left page. Now ask *your* volunteer to insert the playing card or business card into the book and hand it back to *you*.

4 Now here's where *you* must look as if *you*'re doing one thing while *you*'re doing another. You chat with the audience about what has happened so far, and while *you* do this *you* flick through each and every page of the book, talking about how many thousands of words it must contain. You mention how you need your volunteer to continue to think of the last word on the page he selected; otherwise, you'll have little hope of choosing the right word despite your great mental skills.

5 Of course, what you are really doing as you flick through the pages is using the inserted card to your advantage. As you flick, your thumb will briefly stop where the card is inserted. In that brief moment you glance down without moving your head, noting the page number and the last word on either the right or left page

(depending on which one your volunteer was looking at). You must then continue to flick through the pages, talking all the time about your mental skills and your ability to divine other people's thoughts.

6 Once you know the page number and the last word, you should ask your volunteer to try harder to "send" the correct word to you telepathically. After a suitable length of time, you correctly tell the audience the page number and the last word.

7 This trick really relies on your patter and your ability to keep your audience believing you aren't looking through the book! Make sure you practice this one—it seems easy, but it takes skill to make it look very natural.

Trick 72
Linking Minds

★ **You need:** a deck of cards (without the jokers), a table

Your audience will believe *you* really do have magical powers when *you* perform this trick.

1 All you need to do to prepare for this trick is memorize the top card in the deck.

2 Once your audience arrives, spread the deck out facedown on the table. You must keep track of the top card at all times.

3 Explain that you are going to link minds with a volunteer from the audience. Ask for a volunteer to come up and stand before the table. You will call out the name of a card, and she must try to choose the card without looking at the card faces. You need to encourage her by suggesting she take her time and wait until it feels absolutely right.

4 The first card you call out is the card you memorized. Watch to see if your volunteer selects that card. The chances are very good she won't. But whatever card she selects, ask her to hand it to you without looking at it.

MAGIC TRICKS

You now look at it and say something like, "Not bad," and put it to one side, facedown, so no one can see it. The next card you call out is the card you have just seen.

5 The volunteer selects another card and hands it to you, after which you assure her she is doing well and place it facedown on the table with the first card. Call out the name of the just-selected card and have the volunteer look again at the cards, select one, and hand it to you. You again reassure her she is doing well and say you'll try this time.

6 You name the last card you just looked at and say you'll concentrate on that one. You now reach over and pick up the card you memorized—which was also the first one you named. Put it with the rest and scoop up all the cards chosen.

7 For maximum effect, turn them over one by one to see how you and your volunteer both did. Of course, every card is correct.

8 A couple of tips: If at any time your volunteer selects the card you initially memorized, end the trick there and turn over all the cards to show they are correct—don't select one yourself. Another good thing is to have another member of the audience write down the cards you call out, so you can check them later to prove they are all correct.

Trick 73
Hocus-Pocus

★ **You need: a set of dominoes, a calculator**

This trick will show you why math is a magician's best friend! Remember: it's best not to refer to a formula while performing, so memorize the sequence before you begin this trick.

 1 Spread out the set of dominoes on the table and ask a volunteer to choose one. He should not let you see which one he chooses.

 2 Now give him the calculator and ask him to do the following:

Enter one of the domino's numbers.	e.g. 4
Multiply that number by 5.	= 20
Add 7 to the total.	= 27
Double the new total.	= 54
Add the domino's other number to the result.	= 56

3 Finally, ask your volunteer to hand the calculator to you with his answer still showing and say you are adding a bit of hocus-pocus to find out which domino he chose.

 4 As you slowly say the magic words, "Ho-cus-po-cus," press "– 14 =" on the calculator, which in our example would give you an answer of 42. Of course, 4 and 2 are the numbers on the chosen domino!

MAGIC TRICKS

5 If the volunteer had begun his calculation by reversing the numbers (if he began the equation with 2 and added 4 later), the number on the calculator would be 24, as in 2 and 4. If the final answer is a one-digit number, then the other digit is 0.

IT WOULD BE A REALLY BIG HELP IF YOU COULD PICK THAT KNOT UNDONE... ...AHHRR...NO... IT'S NOT PART OF THE TRICK!

Riveting Rope and Ring Tricks

These tricks are good for young people to perform and for their friends to watch. Ropes and rings are easily obtainable in all lengths and colors. Specialty magic shops sell linking rings and every type of magic rope possible, so clever magicians can vary their tricks.

147

Trick 74
The Vanishing Ring

★ **You need:** a rope, a ring, a handkerchief

This is a great, simple trick to begin a routine. It looks like magic, so it must be magic!

1 First, slip the rope through the ring, just as we've shown in the illustration. Make sure the ends of the rope are knotted together so the ring appears trapped.

2 Cover the ring with the handkerchief. Ask a volunteer to hold the knotted ends of the rope while you hold the ring.

3 Now tell your audience you will need all your magical powers to free the ring without untying the rope. Tell the volunteer not to let go of the rope at any cost.

4 Deliver your patter while you keep your hands out of sight behind the handkerchief and push the rope downward over the ring.

SLIDE RING OFF ROPE

5 Utter magical words (whichever ones work best for you) as you free the ring with a flourish, ensuring the rope is still knotted and held by your volunteer. Wait for wild applause!

A TRUE MAGICIAN!!

Trick 75
Two Become One

★ **You need:** a short piece of rope, a longer piece of rope—both the same color and thickness

This is another trick that's easy to learn and execute. It's great to do at the start of a show.

1 You need to prepare your ropes before the audience arrives. Your aim here is for the audience to think you have two ropes of equal length knotted together. That's why the ropes must be the same color and thickness.

TIE SMALL PIECE HERE

SMALL PIECE

2 First, tie the short piece of rope around the center of the long piece. Don't tie it too tightly. Tie the two ends of the long piece together as well. Does it look like you now have two pieces of rope of equal length tied together? If not, redo the knots, because that's the most important part of the trick.

3 Now for your performance. Show the ropes to the audience, holding them carefully in both hands. Tell them you are able, because of your exceptional powers, to make these two short pieces of rope into one long piece.

4 Untie the real knotted ends of the long rope and examine it carefully, making sure to mention the knot in the middle. Now say you're sure you'll be able to get rid of that pesky knot by using a few magic words. You can even ask the audience for their favorite magic words and use one or more of them.

THE PESKY KNOT (The SHORT ROPE)

5 While they are shouting out their magic words, wind the rope around your left hand. Don't stop when you come to the false knot; just hide it as you slide it along the longer rope into your right hand.

SLIDE KNOT ALONG THE LONG ROPE

SIM SALA BIM!

6 Now utter more magic words and unwind the now completely unknotted rope from your left hand. It's now one piece!

MAGIC TRICKS

Trick 76
Knots Away!

★ **You need: a length of rope**

This is a great close-up trick—and the opposite of the previous trick. Now you should tell your audience you want to create knots....

1 First, put the rope across both hands, with your palms up.

2 Now raise the left hand a little, turning it so the palm actually faces you. Do the same with the right hand and a loop forms.

ROUND TWICE MORE

3 Place the loop over your left hand and over the end of the rope that you are holding in your left hand. Allow the rope to pass under your thumb and then return the thumb to its original position.

4 Repeat the looping action twice more and put down the rope (carefully, of course!) and build up an air of expectancy with much talk about concentrating—otherwise the knots won't appear.

5 Slowly lift the rope and, as you do so—if you have performed the trick correctly—three knots will appear by magic. Remember to speak magic words to make the knots appear faster!

So what's going to happen to that pile of stuff?

I have no idea... but I bet it will be fun!

Trick 77
Caught!

★ **You need:** a loop of string, a ring

This is a simple trick, but that doesn't mean it's easy. In this one, you'll catch a ring on a piece of string. You will need to perform a type of throw and flip which needs—yes—practice!

1 Make sure your audience sits directly in front of you for this trick.

2 Hang the loop of string from one hand, stretching it as wide as possible with your fingers spread. Put the ring beneath the loop of string, then lift the ring so that the loop of string is inside it. Position the ring about two-thirds of the way up the loop and hold it with your four fingers above it and your thumb below.

3 Now for the tricky bit: you need to throw the ring hard toward the bottom of the loop and, at the same time, you need to flip the ring so it turns twice and catches in a knot at the bottom of the loop.

THROW RING DOWN AND FLIP!

4 Once the ring is secured in a knot, hold it up to wild applause from your audience.

5 By the way, be prepared to have the ring fall to the floor hundreds of times before you have perfected this trick! Don't give up—it looks wonderful in performance, and your friends will love it!

Look old chap... I can make BIG BEN disappear!

I made the STATUE OF LIBERTY vanish for a full 5 minutes!

When did you see Mt FUJI last?

Did you know?

America, Germany, Japan, and England have produced world-famous magicians. Today, David Copperfield is the magician most people around the world have heard of. He has made a Lear jet disappear! His magic continues to astound.

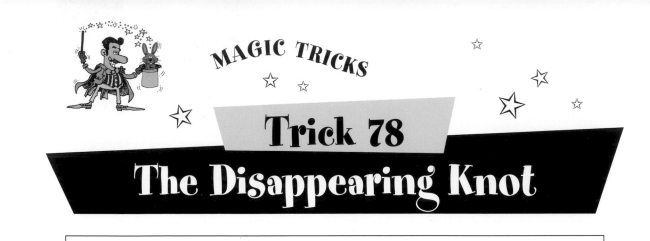

MAGIC TRICKS

Trick 78
The Disappearing Knot

★ **You need:** a piece of thick string (or cord) about 12 in. (30 cm) long, a matchbox cover

This is a terrific trick—your volunteer will believe you can remove a knot from a piece of string, and so will the rest of the audience!

1 Using the illustration as a guide, take the string and use it to tie a single knot around the matchbox cover.

2 Hold the matchbox cover upright and poke one loose string end into the center of the box. Ask a volunteer from your audience to hold the end when it falls through the box.

156

3 Gently—very gently—slide the whole knot off the cover and into the box. Make sure your volunteer is now holding both ends of the string.

4 Here's where the *magic* comes in. Grasp the matchbox cover with your left hand, wave your other hand over the top of it, and say several really great magic words, such as "Alikazam!"

5 With you still holding the matchbox cover, ask the volunteer to gently pull apart the ends of the string (which he is still holding, of course). You can now slide the matchbox cover up and down the string, showing the audience and your volunteer the knot has disappeared!

NO KNOT!

6 Go so far as to hand the matchbox cover and the string to any audience member who wishes to check that your props are genuine!

Riveting Rope and Ring Tricks

Trick 79
Rope Handcuffs

★ **You need:** two 24-in. (60-cm) lengths of cotton rope

You'll tie your audience up in knots with this trick! (Then you'll free them, of course!)

1 Ask for two brave volunteers. Tie their wrists together with the ropes as shown in the illustration.

2 Now ask them to try really hard to release themselves from their predicament without cutting the ropes or untying the knots. Of course, they won't be able to do so, and now you'll have to help them.

3 First, pull the middle of one of the ropes toward the opposite person so you create a loop. Now draw the loop to the wrist of that person, and pass the loop through the rope around the wrist and pull it over the entire hand.

PULL LOOP THROUGH HERE

PULL LOOP OVER AND DOWN

4 Presto! You have freed your volunteers from their rope handcuffs. Ask them to step back from each other and take the wild applause gracefully!

Trick 80
Just One Hand

★ **You need:** one length of rope measuring 35 in. (90 cm)

This is another simple trick that audiences love to watch. You'll tie a knot in a rope using just one hand, and they won't know how you did it!

1 Make sure your audience sits directly in front of you. Now drape the rope across your right palm, between the thumb and index finger and behind the little finger. One end needs to be a little longer than the other (see illustration depicting A and B).

2 Give the rope an upward flick and drop your hand down at the same time. You should catch the longer end of the rope (A) between your index and middle fingers.

3 Now hold onto the A end of the rope between your index and middle fingers and turn your hand so your fingers are pointing toward the floor. The rest of the rope will slip off your hand, forming a one-handed knot!

4 You will have to practice that upward flick—but it's worth it, as it's a classy trick when done correctly!

Oooh... Aye ABRACADABRA! I think we might try a wee rabbit here. This haggis is not really doin' the trick!

Did you know?
Pulling a rabbit out of a hat is supposed to be a classic trick. However, it's a trick that is rarely performed. It was probably devised by Scottish magician John Henry Anderson in the 1830s.

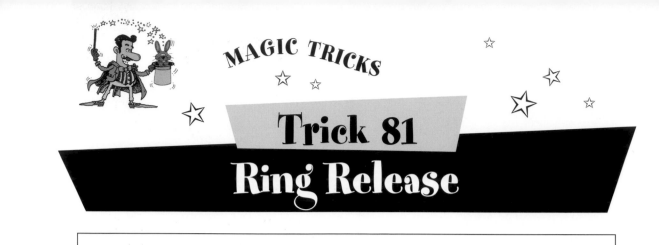

MAGIC TRICKS

Trick 81
Ring Release

★ **You need:** a piece of string 18 in. (45 cm) long, a large ring

In this trick, you'll do the seemingly impossible and remove a large ring that's hanging from a piece of string. Think it sounds simple? Not if you can't slip the ring off either end of the string.

1 Once again, your audience needs to be seated directly in front of you for this trick.

2 Slip the string through the large ring and ask a volunteer to hold one end of the string while you hold the other end. Make sure the string is taut and the ring is in the center of the string.

3 Hold the ring at the bottom and turn it once toward you. Explain you are doing this to lock the ring on the string.

4 Now grasp the string where it joins the ring and drop your end of the string. Put this end of the string through the ring exactly as shown in the illustration.

SPIN

5 Again pull the string taut and tell your audience the ring is now "double locked" on the string.

6 Grasp the ring and flip it so the string is near the bottom of the ring.

7 Finally, grasp the top of the ring and move it quickly back and forth on the string as you pull it toward you. The "locked" ring will come straight off!

163

Trick 82
The Prediction Pendulum Coin

> ★ **You need:** a piece of string, a coin with a hole,
> a large sheet of paper, pencils, a table

You'll know, with the help of your trusty pendulum coin, what your friends have written!

1 Before your show begins, thread the coin on the string.

2 Now for the show—hope you have a large audience! Tear the sheet of paper into eight equal-sized pieces and give the pieces to eight people in your audience. Ask four people to write down the name of an animal and four people to write down the name of a bird.

RRRIP!

3 One of the volunteers can then spread the pieces of paper facedown on the table.

4 Hold the string with the coin above the pieces of paper. Explain to your audience that the coin will swing to and fro over the pieces of paper with animals written on them, but the coin will circle over the pieces of paper containing bird names.

5 Now make the coin swing or circle over each piece of paper, according to what you "see" there, and state whether it's an animal or bird. Immediately turn over the piece of paper to show you're right!

I think I hear a cheep...cheep... under this one!

CHEEP CHEEP

6 You have to be observant and remember two rules when doing this magic trick. First, when you tear the paper, don't use scissors! That's why we said tear it up! The four corner pieces of the sheet of paper will have two smooth edges and two roughly torn edges—these go to the people you ask to write down animal names. The four middle pieces of paper will have three rough edges and one smooth—they go to the people writing bird names. When you do your pendulum predictions, you only have to remember to swing over the paper pieces with two smooth edges, indicating an animal, and circle over the paper pieces with one smooth edge, indicating a bird.

MAGIC TRICKS

Trick 83
The Neverending Rope

★ **You need:** a piece of rope at least 35 in. (90 cm) long, a table, a wand, a jacket with an inside pocket

Your friends won't mind being strung along with this clever rope trick.

1 Show your audience you are holding a short piece of rope. (In fact, you are holding the ends of your long piece of rope, but more on that later.) Explain that your powers can make the rope grow.

2 Tap the back of your hand with your wand, and say some terrific magic words. Then begin to pull the rope from one end. It will continue to grow and grow and grow.

3 You can continue to pull the rope, or even better, ask a volunteer to do so for you. Once it is coiled on the table, take a bow as your audience applauds.

4 How is it done? It's simple, really. Before the show, fold the rope in half and stuff the center into the inside pocket. Thread the rest of the rope up your jacket sleeve and hold both ends in your hand.

MAGIC TRICKS

Trick 84
Cut and Restored Rope

> ★ **You need:** a piece of soft rope about 4 ft. (1.2 m) long, scissors

This is a classic trick all magicians need to perfect. You will appear to cut a piece of rope in half, then restore it.

1 Once more, make sure your audience is seated directly in front of you. Drape the center of the rope over your index finger.

2 Bring one end of the rope up to the middle and tie a square knot.

3 Explain that you have magic scissors—then with a flourish, cut the rope. You must cut it in exactly the place shown in the illustration.

4 Once the cut has been made, casually put the scissors down in a place where the audience cannot see them. Now hold the rope at each end and pull it tightly so everyone can see it's a rope with a knot in the center.

HOLD LITTLE CUT-OFF KNOT INSIDE HAND AS IT SLIDES OFF THE ROPE

5 Begin to wrap the rope around one of your hands—your left if you are right-handed, your right if you are left-handed. As you wrap the rope, the square knot will slide off the rope and must be concealed in your free hand. While you reach for your magic scissors, quickly drop the piece of rope out of sight.

6 Wave your magic scissors over your wrapped hand and recite your favorite magic words. Put down the scissors—this time in full view of your audience—unwrap the rope, and wave it about. The rope is restored!

ABRACADABRA

MAGIC TRICKS

Trick 85
Two Rings and a Rope

★ **You need:** two rings, a piece of rope

You cannot get this trick wrong! It's quick and easy to perform, and you can dazzle the same audience over and over with your magical skills.

1 First, thread the rope through both rings. Tell the audience there are two ways to take the rings off the rope. One, of course, is to slide the rings to the end of the rope. The other is the magic way! You will show them.

2 Use your left thumb and index finger to hold the rope and one ring really firmly at the point marked A in the illustration. Hold the other ring with your right thumb at point B.

3 Quickly pull your right hand down back toward your body and off the end of the rope. This movement will take the ring that was held in your right hand off the rope. At the same time, you will see the ring held in your left hand miraculously pass through the rope as well!

4 Just await the applause! You can do this trick several times for the same audience—they won't be able to see anything but magic!

Fun with Magic

This is what we hope all *your* magic tricks
will lead to: lots of fun. There is no real theme
to the following tricks, as there has been with
the ring, rope, and coin tricks. In fact, the only
thing they have in common is—yes, you've
guessed it—they're fun!

Trick 86
You Can Do What?

★ **You need:** ten magazines (or books) with at least 27 pages each, a calculator, a table

Yes, you can read minds. You'll prove it with this easy trick.

1 To prepare for this trick, place the magazines in a row on the table and study page 27 in the fourth magazine. Check that page for key words or pictures—anything that stands out.

choose
MAGAZINE
Nº 4

2 Give a volunteer the calculator and ask her to do the following:

enter any number between 1 and 100 (for example, 46)

Add 28	= 74
Multiply by 6	= 444
Subtract 3	= 441

Divide by 3	= 147
Subtract 3 more than the original number (46 + 3 = 49)	= 98
Add 8	= 106
Subtract 1 less than the original number (46 – 1 = 45)	= 61
Multiply by 7	= 427

The answer will always be 427!

3 Turn your back to your audience and ask your volunteer to look at the first digit of her calculation. She must not tell you what it is; instead, she should count out that number of magazines.

4 Now ask her to look at the final two digits (27) and to turn to that page in the magazine she has chosen. She should hold that page up to show the audience.

My favorite page in the magazine too!

5 Ask your volunteer and audience to concentrate on what they can see on the page, so you can read their minds. Of course, you'll have no problems, as you have already studied this page. Dazzle your audience by announcing what is on the page!

MAGIC TRICKS

Trick 87
Faster than a Calculator

★ **You need:** a pen or pencil, a piece of paper, a calculator

Amaze your friends (and your parents!) by adding up five three-digit numbers in a few seconds, without using a calculator!

1 There is no need to prepare anything for this trick—you'll use your mental arithmetic skills!

2 Ask a volunteer to write down a three-digit number on the piece of paper. The digits must be different and cannot be consecutive, such as 1, 2, 3.

3 Ask your volunteer to repeat step 2. The two three-digit numbers must be different.

4 Ask for another different three-digit number to be written underneath the first two. This number is the one you are really concerned with—it is the key number.

5 Now you take the pen and paper and write a fourth number from left to right. Make sure the sum of the first and fourth numbers equals 999.

6 Write another number, making sure the sum of the second and fifth numbers equals 999.

7 Give the paper back to your volunteer and ask him to use the calculator to add the five numbers—you are not to see the total.

8 Now, when he returns the paper to you (the total is not written on it), pretend to add up the five numbers in your head within seconds. Write down the total. It will match what he has on the calculator.

MAGIC TRICKS

9 How? Well, remember we said the third number is the key number? It's part of a simple formula, which is:

2000
+ (key number −2)
= the answer

An example:

Volunteer's first number	613
Volunteer's second number	184
Volunteer's third and key number	205
Your number to make 999	386
Your number to make 999	+ 815

= 2203

2000
+ (205−2)
= 2203

10 If your volunteer writes a 9 for the first digit anywhere, add it up to 999, but write down a two-digit number; don't bother with the 0 in front.

Trick 88
In a Tearing Hurry

★ **You need:** two pieces of paper

This is a quick trick you can do only once for an audience—it's a great show opener or can be a bit of light relief after a long trick.

1 Before your audience arrives, make two tears in each of the two pieces of paper, creating three equal strips on each sheet. Do not tear through the sheets completely.

2 Once your audience is seated, ask for a volunteer. Hand your volunteer one of the pieces of paper. Ask her to tear away the two end pieces from the middle piece in just one tear. She won't be able to do it, but you can!

3 Pick up the other piece of paper and show her how it's done. Hold one end piece in each hand. Bend over and hold the middle piece with your lips. Now pull the outside pieces, and you will be left with three separate pieces of paper!

MAGIC TRICKS

Trick 89
The Amazing Jumping Rubber Band

★ **You need:** several colored rubber bands

You only have to learn one secret move in order to perform this simple sleight of hand, but your audience will think you're an amazing magician!

1 Keeping your palm facing you, let the audience see you put a rubber band around the base of your middle and index fingers.

2 Pull the rubber band with your other hand to show that it is solid. As you close your hand, slip all four fingertips inside it. You must do this quickly and secretly. You will need to practice getting all four fingertips into the rubber band with a minimum of movement. When you look at your hand, you can see the rubber band stretched over the four fingers, but the audience will see it stretched around only the first two.

3 Open your hand. The band automatically (and *magically!*) jumps to the other two fingers.

4 Of course, now you want to make it *jump* back again. Put all four fingers into the band as you close your hand; then open your hand. See? The band jumps again. It works every time, once you get the hang of it!

5 If your audience is close to you and you want to vary the trick, use two different-colored rubber bands. Put one rubber band around the base of the middle and index fingers and put the other rubber band around the base of the other two fingers, then put all four fingertips into both. When you open your hand, the bands will *magically* swap places.

Trick 90
The Messy Trick

★ **You need:** three eggs, three cardboard toilet paper rolls, a pie plate, three glasses half-full of water, one broom

In this trick, you're going to make three eggs drop into glasses of water! You'll probably make a mess while you are learning this one, so don't forget to clean up when you've finished practicing!

1 Choose your location—an outside picnic table is a good place to do this trick.

2 Allow your audience to stand around, but not too near, the table.

3 Set up the trick on the edge of the table. The eggs should sit on top of the cardboard rolls (make sure the eggs are the right size; if they are too small or too large to sit properly on the rolls, the trick won't work). The cardboard rolls should sit on the pie plate, and the pie plate should sit on top of the glasses (see illustration). Check that the pie plate is hanging over the edge of the table.

4 Face the table and place the broom in front of you. The bristles of the broom must be directly below the pie plate. You now step on the bristles while pulling the handle of the broom back toward you.

5 As you let go, the handle of the broom will hit the pie plate straight on and things will fly!

6 The three eggs will fall into the half-full glasses of water! Clever magician!

181

MAGIC TRICKS

Trick 91
Stay Awake!

★ **You need:** three or four dark-colored balloons, an equal number of light-colored balloons, string, tape, a pin, a wand

You'll keep audiences awake when you show them how you change the color of a balloon!

1 This trick requires preparation. First, insert your light-colored balloons inside the darker ones. Now inflate each inner (light) balloon, then tie its neck with some string.

2 Now inflate each outer balloon to create an air space between the two balloons. Tie the necks of the outer balloons with the same pieces of string used to tie the inner balloons.

3 Tape a pin to the end of your wand—you want to make a bang! Prick one of the outer balloons and your audience will be amazed to see, and hear, it change color.

BANG

(If you pop both balloons at once, just tell your audience you thought they looked sleepy and they'll miss the next wonderful trick if they doze off!)

4 Hang the balloons around the stage area so you can easily reach them during a performance. Ensure that your audience notices the balloons by referring to them: "I'm surrounded by some fabulous yellow balloons, but I do prefer orange."

5 If you feel the audience is not appreciative enough during any part of your show, touch one of the (outer) balloons with your wand and bang! Not only do people wake up, they realize you've changed the color of the balloon! Pop the balloons throughout your act, ensuring no one sleeps!

No dozing in the back now. Or I may be forced to change the colour of the balloon one more time!

Ooops... I see someone dozing!

183

Trick 92
Fruit or Vegetable?

★ **You need:** a sheet of paper, three pencils, a hat

Sometimes, the simplest tricks are the best. Well, this is one of the best!

1 Prepare for the trick before your audience arrives by tearing a sheet of paper into three equal portions. The trick here is in the tearing—you need to be able to feel the uneven edges of the pieces of paper to enable you to complete the trick. So don't use scissors!

2 Once the audience arrives, ask for three volunteers to come forward to help you with the trick. Hand two volunteers each a piece of paper with only one torn edge (that is, a piece taken from the end of the original sheet), and ask them each to write the name of any fruit on the paper. They are not to show you what they've written.

3 At the same time, hand one volunteer the piece of paper that has two torn sides and ask him to write down the name of a vegetable.

HMMM.... A VEGETABLE

2 TORN SIDES

Try to be casual about which piece of paper you give to each volunteer, but make sure they get the "right" ones!

4 If you have enough members in the audience, ask a fourth volunteer to come forward and place the three pieces of paper into the hat and mix them up.

5 Tell the audience you are able to pull out only the paper with the vegetable named on it. Now reach into the hat, making a big deal out of the fact you can't see the pieces of paper. Feel quickly for the piece of paper with two torn sides, and voilà! There is your vegetable!

MAGIC TRICKS

MAGIC TRICKS

Trick 93
Free-Standing Pencil

★ **You need:** a pencil with an eraser, a push pin

Everything you touch is affected by your magic—you'll prove it by making a pencil stand on its own. Or at least that's what your audience will see, as long as you hide the pin at the end of the trick and don't let audience members get too close!

1 Before the show begins, push the pin into the top of the eraser.

2 Stand in front of your audience and hold up the pencil by the eraser. Hide the pin with your fingers. Say something like: "See, it's just an ordinary pencil, but in my hands it's a magical thing."

3 Bring up your other hand with its palm facing up and, at the same time, turn your body so the side with the hand holding the pencil is facing the audience. (Do this so the audience won't see what you're going to do next.)

While you are turning and your fingers are still hiding the pin from view, place the eraser end of the pencil at the base of the middle and ring fingers of your other hand. The pin slides between these fingers and is held in place by them.

4 Now here comes the magic! Slowly, remove the hand that was originally holding the pencil, preferably while uttering some magic chant, and keep your other hand completely still. It will look as if the pencil is magically standing upright on your palm.

HOCUS-POCUS! SIM SALA BIM!

5 After everyone has had their fill of watching the pencil stand for a few moments, pull the pencil straight up (with a flourish and a bow!) with the other hand. Keep the pin hidden in your fingers.

6 Offer people in the audience a look to assure them it is just an ordinary pencil.

MAGIC TRICKS

Trick 94
Pierce the Potato

★ **You need:** a raw potato with its skin on, some drinking straws

Most people wouldn't believe a flimsy drinking straw could pierce a hard, raw potato—but you know better, right?

1 Get straight into this trick by giving a volunteer the potato and a straw. Challenge her to push the straw into the potato. She will fail, so provide her with some more straws—they'll just crumple and the potato will remain unscathed.

2 However, you know how to do this trick. Take back the potato and say because you have magical powers, your drinking straw is stronger than Kryptonite and can pierce the potato.

3 Secretly fold over the top of the straw and grip it tightly in your fist (see illustration), with the rest of the straw sticking out.

4 Grip the potato in the palm of your other hand.

5 Chant magical words and "embrace" your magical powers, then bring down the straw very quickly, powerfully stabbing the potato. Because of the closed top of the straw, the air within is compressed and makes the straw rigid. Practice your stabbing until the straw goes through the peel and into the potato.

MAGIC TRICKS

Trick 95
What a Corker!

★ **You need:** two equal-sized corks

You'll become a master illusionist with this trick, but be prepared to do many hours of practice! You need to perfect the movements that will convince the audience they are seeing two corks pass through each other!

1 Hold one cork in each hand, in the crooks between your thumbs and index fingers. Have both palms face you.

2 Keep the corks in place, but rotate your writing hand so it is palm-down. Extend the other hand back so it is palm-up.

3 Move your writing hand so it's directly above the other hand. The index finger and thumb of your writing hand (palm-down) should now grip the other hand's cork by placing the index finger on the top of the cork and the thumb on the bottom. At the same time, the index finger and the thumb of the other hand (palm-up) is gripping the cork of the writing hand. To do this, the thumb reaches under the fingers of the writing hand to grip the bottom of the cork, while the index finger reaches under the thumb of the writing hand to grip the top of the cork. It sounds a lot more complicated than it actually is!

4 Now separate your hands, taking away the opposite corks. As your hands move apart, rotate them again—the hand that was palm-down before is now palm-up and the hand that was palm-up is now palm-down.

5 The secret is in practicing this *moving* and *rotating*. When it's done smoothly, it creates the illusion of the two corks passing through each other. Watch yourself in a mirror while you practice—you'll know when you're ready for an audience.

191

MAGIC TRICKS

Trick 96
Coin of Illusion

★ **You need:** a pocketful of change

Although you need many coins for this trick, you use none! Your audience will think you are throwing a coin from hand to hand, but it's all an illusion!

1 Make a show of taking a handful of coins from your pocket. Let the audience see the coins are real. Pretend to choose one coin and pick it up—you'll need to practice this! Return the coins to your pocket.

2 Throw the imaginary coin back and forth from one hand to the other, making a small slapping sound as you pretend to catch the coin each time. Practice with a real coin beforehand so you can get the sound right. Slap the heel of your palm with your fingers as you "catch" your coin, and it should sound as if you're really catching a coin.

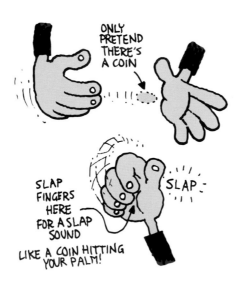

ONLY PRETEND THERE'S A COIN

SLAP FINGERS HERE FOR A SLAP SOUND
LIKE A COIN HITTING YOUR PALM!

SLAP

3 Do this several times, then stop and pretend to hold the imaginary coin in one hand. Ask your audience to guess how it landed: "Heads or tails?" Of course, upon opening your hand, there is no coin. That's OK, because the audience assumes it's now in your other hand.

4 Slowly open your other hand to reveal no coin there either— and bow while your audience applauds!

You should know enough about MAGIC now to know just how I do this trick..! 1... 2....3...

BANG

MAGIC TRICKS

Trick 97
How Many Pieces?

★ **You need:** two strips of paper about 20 in. (50 cm) by 4 in. (10 cm), a black marker, glue

This is a classic destroy-and-restore trick!

1 Before your audience arrives, write the words "ONE PIECE" on each of the two strips of paper. Make the letters look exactly the same on both strips.

2 Fold one strip in half, then in half again, and again—until the paper only measures around 2 in. (5 cm) long and 3 in. (7.5 cm) wide.

3 Glue this tightly folded square to the back of the other strip of paper. Glue it near the end of the strip behind the word "ONE."

4 Now you are ready for an audience. Hold your strip of paper by the ends so the audience sees the words "ONE PIECE." Tell your audience you have just the one piece of paper.

5 Now tear the strip of paper in half. You must be careful not to expose the paper glued on the back. Place the torn-off strip in front of the piece with "ONE" on it and hold them at their smooth ends.

8 SMALL PIECES

6 Say you'd like it smaller, so tear both pieces of paper in half again, putting the pieces of the word "PIECE" in front of the others again. Tear them one last time—by now making lots of fun of the words "ONE PIECE." You should now have eight pieces.

7 Fold the pieces, keeping the edges away from you and even with the secret folded piece of paper. Are you holding a packet of folded paper between your fingers and thumb of your right hand? You should be. The audience only sees torn pieces of paper but you can see one whole strip.

8 Look confused, and say something like: "But now I've done this, I really think I prefer it as one piece." As you say this, pass the folded packet over to your left hand and turn it around. The strip that is still in one piece should now be facing the audience.

MAGIC TRICKS

9 Once your fingers and thumb have secured the packet, wave your hand over it and chant a few magic words. Now, dramatically open the strip so the audience can see the words "ONE PIECE," apparently whole again!

HOLD TORN PIECES BEHIND HERE

ONE PIECE

10 The torn pieces are folded together so they shouldn't separate and fall to the floor. If they do, keep practicing!

Trick 98
Any Color

★ **You need: three different-colored crayons, a table**

You can choose the correct-colored crayon every time—without looking!

1 Prepare for this trick by marking each of the crayons in a different way. You need to be able to tell which crayon is which just by feeling them. The marks, of course, cannot be obvious to anyone looking at the crayons. So, for instance, you might tear a piece of the paper from one, make a nick in the bottom of another with your fingernail or a pair of scissors, and make a nick in the top of the third one. Only you know which mark matches which color, and, naturally, you must remember this!

2 With this trick, it's important to be dramatic! You don't want your audience to notice that you are feeling for the mark on a particular crayon, so you need to distract them. Talk to your audience and explain that you're concentrating hard, trying to "sense" the colors.

MAGIC TRICKS

3 To perform the trick, turn away from your audience and ask a volunteer to randomly place the crayons into your hands, which you are holding behind your back.

4 Now face your audience and ask the volunteer to call out one of the colors. Start acting, while you feel for the mark of the particular color called.

RED

5 When you find the crayon, bring it out with a flourish and wait for the applause. Do this trick only once or twice in a show.

THAT LOOKS LIKE RED TO ME...! DO I HAVE EYES ON THE BACK OF MY HEAD?

Trick 99
Hidey Ho

★ **You need:** a deck of cards, a large scarf (or handkerchief)

You're such a good magician that any card you name can penetrate a solid object, such as a scarf!

1 All you have to do beforehand is secretly memorize the top card in the facedown deck and then remember not to shuffle the cards!

MEMORIZED CARD NOW ON BOTTOM OF DECK

2 Hold the deck faceup in the palm of your left hand if you're right-handed, or in your right if you are left-handed. The card you have memorized should be sitting on the bottom of the deck in your palm.

3 Show the scarf to the audience—in fact, pass it around so everyone can see it's an ordinary scarf.

4 Once it's returned to you, drape the scarf over the deck of cards so its center rests on top of the deck.

MAGIC TRICKS

5 Make sure you draw the audience's attention to the fact you now can't see the cards. Now, reach under the scarf with your other hand and remove the deck, but leave the bottom, memorized card behind in your palm.

MEMORIZED CARD

6 Place the deck of cards on top of the scarf, directly over the card that is hidden under the scarf.

7 Begin to wrap the scarf around the deck of cards. Start by folding the edge nearest to you away from you with your free hand. Place the thumb of this hand underneath the memorized card and the wrapped deck. Place the rest of the fingers on top to grip the deck, and now rotate it upright so the hidden card faces you. Do this part carefully, because if you allow the hidden card to shift, the audience will see it!

8 Now, keeping the hand gripping the deck where it is, use your opposite hand to fold the sides of the scarf back toward you, diagonally over the hidden card. The folds need to overlap this card, while your thumb holds everything in place.

9 It's time to dazzle your audience! With the fist of the hand that folded the scarf, grip all of the scarf hanging below and rotate the deck (keeping the hidden card facing you) so it is hanging down. If the folds are tight enough, the hidden card should stay in place when you lift your thumb.

10 Tell your audience that you can magically make any card you call appear through the scarf. Now, of course, you call the card you have memorized—the hidden card—and then shake the deck, while chanting magic words. The hidden card will magically begin to appear as if it is penetrating the center of the scarf. When it hits the table, allow the wrapped deck to be examined as you bask in your audience's admiration!

Trick 100
Counting Cards

★ **You need:** a deck of cards

This is a simple "find the card" trick that works on its own, but you can make it yours with some cleverly planned patter.

10 CARDS

1 Count out the top 10 cards from a deck of cards, but don't let your audience guess that you are counting. Use some patter to distract the audience while you set up the trick.

2 When you've counted out 10 cards, sweep them up and return them to the top of the deck, secretly glancing at the bottom card—let's say it's the eight of spades.

MEMORIZE THIS CARD!

3 Ask the audience, or a volunteer in the audience, for a number between 10 and 19. If the number you're given is 14, for example, you count out 14 cards on the table.

14 CARDS

4 Put the rest of the deck to one side and add the digits of the chosen number, 1 and 4, together. You get 5.

5 Announce what you think the fifth card is (here, the memorized card, the eight of spades). Deal out five cards from the small pile, and the fifth card will be the eight of spades!

SMALL PILE

5th CARD will be 8 of SPADES

Trick 101
A No-Card Card Trick

★ **You need:** nothing but your mind
and some good patter

Finally, here's a card trick you can perform when you don't have a deck of cards handy.

1 Ask a volunteer to name a number between one and ten, then tell him he should change his mind and choose another number! He mustn't tell anyone the second number, but ask him to double it.

2 Now, ask him to add 14 to it; then divide by 2; then subtract the original number. The answer is the value of his imaginary card. He must remember it.

3 For example:

First choice	3
Second number	4
Double it	8
Add 14	22
Divide by 2	11
Subtract original	(− 4)7

4 Now ask him to concentrate on a suit of cards—either hearts, clubs, diamonds, or spades. You pretend to concentrate and then blurt out a suit, for instance, "Diamonds."

5 It is unlikely your first guess will be right, so keep guessing until you name the right suit.

6 Of course, the audience now thinks you're having trouble with the trick, as you probably took a few guesses to get the right suit. But, as soon as you guess the suit, you say something like: "Boy, I can't believe you chose the seven of hearts [or whatever]."

7 Pause here—you need your volunteer to realize you have chosen the correct value of the card. Then he can tell the audience how clever you are.

8 This is really a simple trick. If you ask your volunteer to add 14, the final number will be 7; if you ask him to add 10, the final number will be 5; and so on. The answer is always going to be half of the number you ask him to add.

You're the greatest magician I know!

MAGIC TRICKS